THE MONTESSORI WAY

An Education for Life
A Comprehensive Guide for Parents and Teachers

Tim Seldin • Dr. Paul Epstein • Dr. Robin Howe

Montessori
FOUNDATION

QUARRY

Quarto.com

© 2025 Quarto Publishing Group USA Inc.
Text, Photos © 2025 Montessori Foundation Inc.

First Published in 2025 by Quarry Books, an imprint of The Quarto Group,
100 Cummings Center, Suite 265-D, Beverly, MA 01915, USA.
T (978) 282-9590 F (978) 283-2742

Quarry Books titles are also available at discount for retail, wholesale, promotional, and bulk purchase. For details, contact the Special Sales Manager by email at specialsales@quarto.com or by mail at The Quarto Group, Attn: Special Sales Manager, 100 Cummings Center, Suite 265-D, Beverly, MA 01915, USA.

10 9 8 7 6 5 4 3 2 1

ISBN: 978-0-7603-9277-5

Digital edition published in 2025
eISBN: 978-0-7603-9278-2

Library of Congress Cataloging-in-Publication Data

Names: Seldin, Tim, 1946- author.
Title: The Montessori way : an education for life; a comprehensive guide
  for parents and teachers / Tim Seldin, Dr. Paul Epstein, Dr. Robin Howe.
Identifiers: LCCN 2024049043 (print) | LCCN 2024049044 (ebook)
  | ISBN 9780760392775 (trade paperback) | ISBN 9780760392782 (ebook)
Subjects: LCSH: Montessori method of education.
Classification: LCC LB1029.M75 S46 2025 (print) | LCC LB1029.M75 (ebook)
  | DDC 371.39/2—dc23/eng/20241101
LC record available at https://lccn.loc.gov/2024049043
LC ebook record available at https://lccn.loc.gov/2024049044

Design and Page Layout: Cindy Samargia Laun
Cover Image: Glenn Scott Photography
Photography: Montessori Foundation Inc., except Association
  Montessori Internationale on pages 20, 22, 26, 29, 30, and 32
  and Shutterstock on pages 10, 68, and 186.
Montessori products featured on cover and pages 4, 49, 52, 76, 191–193,
  and 206 are courtesy of Nienhuis (www.nienhuis.com).

Printed in China

The last few years have been a time of challenge, change, and opportunity. Dr. Montessori's vision, mission, and work are more important than ever.

Our world is at a crossroads, perhaps a tipping point. A few years ago, we experienced the shared trauma of a global pandemic. Conflict, climate change, technological advancements, artificial intelligence, and other discoveries on the horizon have left many families concerned and confused.

More families than ever around the world are choosing to homeschool their children or seek schools that feel different to give them a better sense that their children will be safe, nurtured, and encouraged to think outside the box, think deeply, and think about others.

Increasingly, Dr. Montessori is seen as one of the important voices for meaningful change. Tens of thousands of Montessori schools exist in more than 110 countries. Her books have been translated into most languages and attract interest among educators and parents to open new schools based on her work.

Having lived through two world wars as a global citizen, Maria Montessori urged us to "light a candle rather than curse the darkness."

How fortunate that Montessori provides us with a replicable, adaptable, sustainable platform to build more peaceful and harmonious schools, organizations, and homes.

This book was first published in 2003 through an extraordinarily generous contribution by Tony Low-Beer, a wonderful man who provided encouragement and support to the Montessori Foundation.

The authors wish to express their deepest appreciation to Mr. Low-Beer and his family.

We also thank the schools that invited our brilliant photographer, Larry Canner, into their classrooms to capture children going about their lives from infancy through high school. Those schools include the Desert Garden Montessori School and the Keystone Montessori Charter School of Phoenix, Arizona; Love of Learning Montessori School in Columbia, Maryland; Montessori School of Central Maryland; The Montessori School of Raleigh in Raleigh, North Carolina; Kingsley Montessori School of Boston, Massachusetts; The NewGate School of Sarasota, Florida; and the Westwood School of Dallas, Texas.

We also thank the Association Montessori Internationale for allowing us to share some of the many photographs in its archives.

Finally, this book is dedicated to Joyce St. Giermaine, the Executive Director of the Montessori Foundation, and our terrific staff, who helps to spread the insights and approach to educating the world's children that Dr. Maria Montessori developed.

The years ahead hold the promise of a stronger global community and a new sense of our common humanity and shared destiny.

This can and must be the period in human history when we build new patterns of collaboration, partnership, and trust.

As always, it begins with us.

Paul Epstein
Robin Howe
Tim Seldin

Contents

Foreword

What is education for? How we answer this question is critical for the future of our children, our nation, and our world. Yet, all too often, it gets lost in debates about standards, testing, and other procedural reforms that treat education as something to be done to children rather than for and with them.

The Montessori Way shows that we can, and must, go back to basics—to the real purpose of education as drawing forth from each of us our full human potential. It is a highly practical book. But it is much more than that. It describes a way of life—a way of thinking about the nature of intelligence, talent, and the potential for goodness and greatness among all people—a way to nurture and inspire creativity, curiosity, leadership, love, and imagination that lies within us all. It reminds us that the child is the parent of the adult they will one day become and that the most important human task is to nurture and educate children.

Based on Dr. Maria Montessori's pioneering work and more recent knowledge about how children develop, learn, and access their full humanity, *The Montessori Way* embodies partnership education, which is designed not only to help young people better navigate through our difficult times but also to help them create a more peaceful, equitable, and sustainable future.

Rather than relying on a paradigm of domination and submission, of winning and losing, of external rewards and punishments, of top-down rankings, fear, manipulation, indoctrination, and pressure to conform, *The Montessori Way* presents an education that focuses on partnership, independence, mutual trust, and respect, on both individual achievement and collaboration, while developing our minds and hearts.

Education explicitly or implicitly gives young people a mental map of what it means to be human. Much of what young people worldwide learn through formal and informal education holds up a distorted mirror of themselves. When their vision of the future comes out of this limited worldview, they cannot develop their full humanity or meet the unprecedented challenges they face.

In *The Montessori Way*, Tim Seldin, Paul Epstein, and Robin Howe offer sound guidelines, practical tools, and inspiring real-life stories of how, working together, teachers, children, parents, and others can create learning communities where everyone can feel safe and seen for who we truly are, where our essential humanity and that of others shines through, lifting our hearts and spirits, and empowering us to realize our highest intellectual, emotional, and spiritual potentials.

In her unshakable faith in the human spirit and her fearless challenge to traditions of domination, Dr. Montessori is one of my role models. Her legacy, as expanded and enriched by countless others, is the gift of this wonderful book.

Riane Eisler
Carmel, California

Riane Eisler is the author of many books, including *The Chalice and the Blade*, *Sacred Pleasures*, *Nurturing Our Humanity*, *Tomorrow's Children: A Blueprint for Partnership Education in the 21st Century*, *The Real Wealth of Nations*, *The Power of Partnership*, and *The Partnership Way*.

Introduction

I do not believe there is a method better than Montessori for making children sensitive to the beauties of the world and awakening their curiosity regarding the secrets of life.

—Gabriel García Márquez: author, Nobel laureate, and Montessori alumnus

The Montessori Way offers a comprehensive and well-illustrated introduction to the educational programs that evolved from the work of Dr. Maria Montessori (1870–1952). We wrote this book with several audiences in mind, from parents and grandparents who want to understand what makes Montessori special to educators seeking a comprehensive introduction to this important movement in school reform.

Even though we work with and appreciate the full scope of educational movements in the United States and abroad, we are passionate about Montessori education. Dr. Montessori was a genius, and many others with genius have developed innovations in helping children learn. We particularly acknowledge contemporary movements such as Waldorf and Reggio Emilia education. There are many other approaches that put the child in the center rather than the teacher. We call them all, including Montessori, "child honoring." Montessori is distinct because it is less dependent on the teacher's personality. Dr. Montessori was a scientist whose methods were systematic, coherent, replicable, adaptable, and sustainable. We have more than 22,000 Montessori schools in the world, some of which have been running for almost a hundred years. The movement has stood the test of time.

Some Montessori schools only offer early childhood programs; others offer programs from the infant-toddler level up through early childhood, elementary, or even secondary. Most are private or independent schools founded by an individual teacher or a parent board. There are a growing number of public school programs, and many homeschools implement aspects of the Montessori approach.

Since the Montessori Foundation first published *The Montessori Way*, the fundamental themes and practices of Montessori have changed very little. As Montessori programs have grown and spread throughout the world, though, the curriculum is practiced in more varied environments and schools than ever before.

Academic research over the past few decades has also given us further evidence of the benefits and outcomes demonstrated by Montessori students. More and more parents and teachers are curious to learn more, and we hope that this book will provide a clear, concise explanation of the history, practice, and essential elements of Montessori.

PART ONE

Philosophy and Influence

CHAPTER 1

Montessori:
The Common Principles

Each of the 22,000 Montessori schools around the world is built on the educational legacy of Dr. Montessori and her influential work.

Since 1907, the year of her first school, children and adults have engaged in an approach to learning that addresses all aspects of growth: cognitive, physical, social, emotional, and spiritual. In Montessori schools worldwide, children develop the habits and skills of lifelong learning.

Although Montessori schools may appear different, they share a common philosophy and fundamental approach. The Montessori approach has four great qualities: This educational model is replicable; it can be successfully adapted to new situations; it can include educational innovations based on recent understandings of learning; and it is sustainable, operating continuously in many schools for decades.

Montessori is more than a child-centered educational approach. It organizes human relationships and institutions that lead people toward partnership and great levels of personal satisfaction and harmony. Montessori is a way of life that can be expressed in loving relationships, child-rearing and family life, friendships, classrooms, the workplace, leadership, and civic life.

All Montessori schools follow five common principles based on Dr. Montessori's research and methods.

FIVE COMMON PRINCIPLES OF MONTESSORI SCHOOLS

1. An educational partnership between teachers and students.

Guided by teachers who are trained to observe and identify children's unique learning capabilities, students learn in a culture of partnerships with their teachers. This method of instruction involves observation and development of learning environments in which teachers challenge children to extend their unique style of learning fully. Because children's interests are heard and honored, Montessori students develop confidence and become self-directed. Due to this self-directed, self-initiated orientation to learning, a powerful learning formula emerges. When interested, a child becomes self-motivated. Self-motivation leads to self-discipline, or correcting or improving oneself without external motivation. Self-disciplined children engage in mastery learning and fully develop their potential.

2. Honoring the true nature of childhood.

We know that children are complete individuals in their own right. Even when very small, children deserve to be treated with the full and sincere respect that would be extended to their parents. Respect breeds respect and creates an atmosphere within which learning is tremendously facilitated.

Dr. Montessori developed her unique approach to education, recognizing and honoring how children naturally learn and grow. It is based on the hidden secrets of child development: physical, social, intellectual, and psychological.

3. Discovery, cooperation, kindness, and nonviolence.

Montessori educators work with infants, toddlers, young children, and adolescents. We see an inherent tendency toward discovery, cooperation, kindness, and nonviolence at each age.

Each day, in Montessori schools throughout the world, children exhibit the vast wonder of the human spirit, the endless faces of intelligence, creativity, and inventiveness. Montessori schools inspire a kinder, more pleasant, productive, and peaceful world than most humans have ever known or imagined.

4. All children are uniquely intelligent.

In 1907, Dr. Montessori discerned a fundamental premise about children and humanity: All children have unique potential. This premise challenged long-held beliefs about intelligence and the inherent nature of humanity as violent and competitive.

Montessori believed that intelligence is not fixed at birth and that human potential is unlimited. The research of Jean Piaget, Howard Gardner, Daniel Goleman, and many others has confirmed the validity of this belief.

Whereas Montessori wrote about unique, individual potential, it is more fashionable today to discuss each person's *multiple intelligences*.

5. Measuring outcomes in Montessori.

The Montessori Way starkly contrasts with the current fervor to evaluate teachers by how well children perform on standardized tests. In Montessori, we focus on observation and assessing what children understand and can accomplish. We follow the child, rather than assuming that all students will learn a specific set of skills at the same pace.

At traditional schools, teaching to the test and rehearsed test taking may result in schools with test scores that reward adults with jobs and funding. But under this regime, too many children are denied music, art, physical education, recess, and even science and history.

Current brain research suggests that learning environments should be stimulating, relaxed, intriguing, and safe for exploration. Once a child is free from stress, then thinking, problem-solving, and forming trusting relationships are all possible. To learn more about scientific research on Montessori, see the appendix.

CHAPTER 2

Montessori's Influence on Education

Dr. Maria Montessori is as controversial a figure in education today as she was in the first half of the twentieth century. Alternately heralded as one of the last century's leading advocates for early childhood education or dismissed as outdated and irrelevant, her research and the studies she inspired helped change the course of education.

Many noted psychologists studied with her and were influenced by her work, including Anna Freud, Jean Piaget, Alfred Adler, and Erik Erikson. They then went on to make their own contributions to education and child psychology.

Perhaps the most obvious way Dr. Montessori reshaped our understanding of children and schooling was her recognition of the importance of the first six years of life in shaping a child's long-term development. Her discovery of the correlation between early brain stimulation through language, movement, exploration, freedom to discover, basic cultural literacy, and eye, hand, and gross-muscle development still influences every early childhood classroom.

Dr. Maria Montessori (1870–1952)

While Dr. Montessori did not work in isolation, and other researchers studied child development before and after her time, she spotlighted early childhood education and the importance of helping parents understand their children and better support their social, emotional, and intellectual development.

As James Heckman pointed out in his Nobel-winning research, an investment in early childhood education pays excellent dividends. Montessori demonstrated that children are capable of amazing things. With the proper stimulation, we can nurture brain development and human potential tangibly, especially for families of less privilege.

The highest rate of return in early childhood development comes from investing in disadvantaged families as early as possible, from birth through age five. Starting at age three or four is too little too late, as it fails to recognize that skills beget skills in a complementary and dynamic way. Efforts should focus on the first years for the greatest efficiency and effectiveness.

—James Heckman, December 7, 2012

SECURITY, SELF-WORTH, PARTNERSHIP, AND CHOICE

While there is still tremendous variation in how schools approach children's learning and development and most classrooms are still largely teacher-centered, Dr. Montessori demonstrated the importance of giving children a sense of agency and choice. Schools moved from a norm in which children sat still at their desks, which were screwed to the floor, almost all day long, and followed a teacher-prescribed schedule to an approach that recognizes the value of giving students some choice and freedom to move around the classroom.

Dr. Montessori also recognized the obvious truth that children learn in different ways and at different paces. Her approach led to what we now call *individualized education* and *differentiated instruction*.

She taught teachers to observe what children are doing, what interests them, and how they understand how things work. This deeper look into how children think and learn led to what we now call a constructivist approach to education, made even more popular by influential psychologists such as Jean Piaget and Lev Vygotsky.

Dr. Montessori recognized the correlation between a child's sense of security and self-worth and their ability to learn. Again, while she certainly was not the only person working in social-emotional learning and child guidance, Dr. Montessori pioneered the idea of a partnership among parents, schools, and children.

PREPARED LEARNING ENVIRONMENTS

Dr. Montessori's prepared learning environments set the stage for psychologists and educators to recognize that children construct their understanding of the world through interacting with it. Hands-on learning and a discovery approach are now widely recognized, if not always practiced, in classrooms around the world.

Her recognition of the value of designing school furniture and everyday items, from sinks and toilets to basic tools, to fit the size of the child, was groundbreaking in its time and is almost taken for granted today.

The way Dr. Montessori organized materials for learning created a concept of curricular sequence and order that is invaluable in facilitating and

The sandpaper letters, one of the hundreds of Montessori learning materials

increasing student independence, choice, ability to discover their own mistakes, and many of the self-organizing and self-regulating principles that we now call executive-function skills. The beauty of her learning environments and the deliberate attempt to avoid overstimulation and interruptions in children's concentration is certainly recognized by people who pay attention to such things.

MONTESSORI MATERIALS

In designing her world-famous learning materials, Dr. Montessori deliberately built in what she called a *control of error*, which allows children to discover their own mistakes. This groundbreaking idea continues to influence cutting-edge education today.

Dr. Montessori also developed and made common many other things among Montessori schools all over the world. One example is the concept of a pattern language in the materials that make up

the early-childhood through elementary curriculum. This concept uses carefully designed color-coding and sequencing to create a recognizable look and feel to a Montessori classroom that goes above and beyond the furniture, the clutter-free classroom walls, how children move around the room, and the learning materials.

Many elements of modern education have been adapted from Dr. Montessori's theories. She is credited with developing the open classroom, the role of the teacher as a guide, multi-age classrooms, developmentally appropriate and individualized education, and the use of manipulative learning materials. Educators around the world have begun to recognize the consistency between the Montessori approach and what we continue to learn from research in child development, brain science, and best practices in teaching. Dr. Montessori was an individual ahead of her time.

PART TWO

History of the Montessori Movement

CHAPTER 3

Dr. Maria Montessori

Maria Montessori was born in 1870 in Chiaravalle, Italy, to an educated middle-class family. She grew up in a country considered conservative in its attitude toward women. Despite considerable opposition from her father and her teachers, Dr. Montessori pursued a scientific education and was one of the first women to become a physician in Italy.

To aid life, leaving it free, however, to unfold itself, that is the essential task of the educator.

—Dr. Maria Montessori

Dr. Maria Montessori, 1933

As a practicing physician, she was a scientist, not a teacher. It is ironic that she became famous for her contributions to a field that she had rejected as the traditional refuge for women at a time when few professions were open to them.

Dr. Montessori specialized in pediatrics and psychiatry. She taught at the University of Rome medical school, and through its free clinics, she frequently contacted the working class and poor children. These experiences convinced her that intelligence is not rare and that most children come into the world with a human potential that is barely revealed—unless adults create environments specifically designed for children to exercise their learning capabilities. Her work reinforced her humanistic ideals, and she made time to support various social reform movements. Early in her career, she began to accept speaking engagements throughout Europe for the women's movement, peace efforts, and child labor law reform. Dr. Montessori became well-known and highly regarded throughout Europe.

In 1900, Dr. Montessori was appointed director of the new orthophrenic school attached to the University of Rome. An orthophrenic school is designed for children with significant emotional or behavioral challenges, addressing both academic and psychological needs. Children at the school were probably developmentally delayed or autistic. She initiated reforms in a system that had formerly confined youngsters with cognitive delays in empty rooms. Dr. Montessori recognized her patients' need for stimulation, purposeful activity, and self-esteem, so she insisted that staff speak to each child with the highest respect. She created a program to teach her young charges how to care for themselves and their environment.

At the same time, she began a meticulous study of the available research on learning and teaching. Swiss philosopher Jean-Jacques Rousseau (1712–1778) believed sensory experience was the basis for all knowledge. He argued that teachers must begin with knowing learners and that a teacher's role is to assist learners to fully develop their own natures. To do this, teachers must begin with concrete, sensory experiences rather than lecture-based recitations. From the Swiss educational reformer Johann Heinrich Pestalozzi (1746–1827), Dr. Montessori found further support for the idea that teachers develop the capabilities of learners rather than impart information. Pestalozzi defined observation as the method of teaching. His curriculum was based on engaging children in direct experiences involving physical activity, making connections, and going on outings beyond the classroom. He sequenced learning experiences from simple to complex and from concrete to abstract.

Friedrich Froebel (1782–1852), the German educator and originator of the kindergarten, bridged the ideas of Pestalozzi and Rousseau. Froebel studied with Pestalozzi from 1806 to 1810 before opening his own school in 1816. Froebel believed that education was a process of self-activity and self-discovery, leading to self-fulfillment.

For Froebel, the goal of an educator was to discover the universal principles that guided this process. Teachers should guide, not coerce, and they should never interfere with children's spontaneous learning activities. Froebel developed a series of "gifts," or play materials, including balls, cubes, cylinders, and blocks, which heightened children's awareness of relationships among things.

Dr. Montessori also studied two almost-forgotten French physicians of the eighteenth and nineteenth centuries: Jean Marc Gaspard Itard (1774–1838) and Édouard Séguin (1812–1880).

Itard is most famous for his work with the "wild boy of Aveyron," a youth found wandering naked in the forest, having spent ten years living alone. The boy could not speak and lacked almost all everyday life skills. Scientists of the time argued that here was a "natural man," a human being who had developed without the benefit of culture and socialization with his kind. Itard hoped that this study would shed light on the age-old debate about what proportion of human intelligence and personality is hereditary and what proportion stems from learned behavior.

The experiment had limited success, for Itard found the boy unable to cooperate or learn most things. This led Itard to postulate the existence of developmental periods in normal human growth. During these "sensitive periods," a child must experience stimulation or grow up forever lacking the adult skills and intellectual concepts he missed at the stage when they can be readily learned!

Although Itard's efforts to teach the boy were barely successful, he systematically designed a pedagogical process, arguing that all education would benefit from careful observation and experimentation.

This idea had tremendous appeal to the scientifically trained Dr. Montessori and later became a cornerstone of her method. Séguin, one of Itard's students, carried his work further, developing a far more specific and organized system for applying it to the everyday education of children with disabilities.

Séguin is recognized as a father of modern special education techniques. He outlined an active sensory education that included graduated exercises in motor education, sorting geometric shapes, and explorations of textures, colors, and sizes.

From these predecessors, Dr. Montessori refined the idea of a scientific approach to education based on observation and experimentation. She belongs to the "child-study" school of thought, and she pursued her work with the careful training and objectivity of a biologist studying an animal's natural behavior in the forest. She studied children with special learning needs, listening and carefully noting everything they did and said, as well as which teaching methods worked best.

CHAPTER 4

The San Lorenzo Discoveries

The Italian Ministry of Education did not welcome Dr. Montessori's suggestion that her methodology, which had worked well with children with special learning needs, would yield even more dramatic results when used with other children. Consequently, she was unable to continue the experiment with children in the state schools. Several years later, in 1907, Dr. Montessori accepted an invitation to coordinate a daycare center for the children of working-class parents—children who were too young to attend public school. This first *Casa dei Bambini*, or Children's House, was located in San Lorenzo, an impoverished district of Rome. The conditions were appalling. Her first class included more than fifty children from ages two through seven, taught by one untrained caregiver.

The 1908 opening of the Montessori Children's House in Milan

The children remained at the center from dawn to dusk while their parents worked. They were fed two meals daily, bathed regularly, and given medical care. The children themselves were typical of extreme inner-city poverty conditions.

On the first day, they entered the Children's House crying and pushing, exhibiting aggressive and impatient behavior.

On that day, there was nothing to be seen but about fifty wretchedly poor children, rough and shy in manner, many of them crying, almost all the children of illiterate parents who had been entrusted to my care.

They were tearful, frightened children, so shy that it was impossible to get them to speak. Their faces were expressionless, and their bewildered eyes seemed as though they had never seen anything in their lives.

—Dr. Maria Montessori

Not knowing whether her methods would work under such conditions, Dr. Montessori began by teaching the older children how to help with the everyday tasks that needed to be done. She also introduced the manipulative perceptual puzzles she had used with children with developmental delays.

I brought them some of the materials used for our work in experimental psychology, the items we use today as sensorial material, and materials for practical life exercises. I merely wanted to study the children's reactions. I asked the woman in charge not to interfere with them in any way; otherwise, I would not be able to observe them . . . No one loved them. I myself only visited them once a week, and during the day, the children had no communication with their parents . . .

But most beautiful of all was the fact that they had interesting occupations in which no one, no one at all, interfered. They were left alone, and little by little, the children began to work with concentration, and the transformation they underwent was noticeable. From timid and wild as they were before, the children became sociable and communicative. Their personalities grew, and strange though it may seem, they showed extraordinary understanding, activity, vivacity, and confidence. They were happy and joyous.

—Dr. Maria Montessori

Students working in one of the first Children's Houses, 1907

The results surprised her. Unlike her earlier experiences coaxing children to use the learning materials, the children of San Lorenzo were drawn to the work she introduced. Children who had wandered aimlessly the previous week began to settle down to long periods of constructive activity. They were fascinated with the puzzles and perceptual training devices. To Dr. Montessori's amazement, three- and four-year-old children were delighted to learn practical, everyday living skills that reinforced their independence and self-respect.

Soon, the older children took care of the school, assisted their teacher with preparing and serving meals, maintained a spotless environment, and even learned to read and write. Their behavior as a group changed dramatically, from wild street urchins to models of grace and courtesy.

Children serving the midday meal in Rome, 1908

OBSERVING THE DESIRE TO LEARN

Dr. Montessori paid close attention to the children's spontaneous behavior, arguing that only in this way could a teacher know how to teach. Traditionally, schools had paid little attention to children as individuals. Instead, they demanded that students adapt to the school's standards. Dr. Montessori believed that the educator's job was to serve the child, determining what each one needed to make the most significant progress. To her, a child who failed in school should not be blamed, any more than a doctor should blame a patient who does not get well fast enough.

Dr. Montessori's children learned to read and write quickly and enthusiastically. They were also fascinated by numbers. The mathematically inclined Dr. Montessori developed a series of concrete math learning materials that have never been surpassed.

Six months after the inauguration of the House of Children, some of the mothers came to me. They pleaded that as they themselves were illiterate, would I not teach their children to read and write?

At first, I did not want to, being as prejudiced as everyone else, that the children were far too young for it. But I gave them the alphabet. I analyzed the words for them and showed that each sound of the words had a symbol by which it could be materialized. It was then that the explosion into writing occurred.

—**Dr. Maria Montessori**

Soon, her four- and five-year-old students were performing four-digit addition and subtraction operations and, in many cases, pushing on even further. Their interests blossomed in other areas, compelling an overworked physician to spend night after night designing new materials to keep pace with the children's interest in geometry, geography, history, and natural science. The final proof of the children's desires came soon after her first school became famous, when a group of well-intentioned women gave them a marvelous collection of lovely and expensive toys. The new gifts held the children's attention for a few days, but the students soon returned to the more interesting learning materials. To Dr. Montessori's surprise, children preferred work over play most of the time.

Dr. Montessori evolved her method through trial and error. She told of the morning when the teacher arrived late to find that the children had crawled through a window and gone right to work. In the beginning, the learning materials were expensive, handmade, and locked away in a cabinet. Only the teacher had a key. In this instance, the teacher had neglected to lock the cabinet the night before.

Finding it open, the children selected one material apiece and worked quietly. When Dr. Montessori arrived, the teacher was scolding the children for taking the materials without permission. Dr. Montessori recognized that the children were capable of selecting their own work. She removed the cabinet and replaced it with low, open shelves. This may sound like a minor change today, but it contradicted all educational practices and theories of that period.

DISCOVERY

Dr. Montessori did not see the core of her work as a method or curriculum, per se, but as a dramatic discovery that children around the world share universal characteristics and tendencies, even as each child is a unique human being who deserves the same respect we would give an adult.

One discovery followed another. She found that young children enjoyed long periods of quiet concentration, though they rarely showed signs of it in everyday settings. Although they were often careless and sloppy, they responded positively to an atmosphere of calm and order. Dr. Montessori noticed that the logical extension of the young child's love for routine is an environment in which everything has a place. Her children took tremendous delight in carefully carrying their work to and from the shelves, taking great pains not to spill or bump into anything. They walked carefully through the room instead of running, as they did on the streets. The environment itself was an essential component.

After recognizing the frustration that a small child experiences in an adult-sized world, Dr. Montessori had carpenters build child-sized tables and chairs. Eventually, she designed entire schools around the children's size. She prepared miniature pitchers and bowls and found forks and knives that fit a child's tiny hand. The tables were lightweight, allowing two children to move them without adult assistance. The children learned to control their movements, disliking the way their calm was disturbed when they knocked into things.

Dr. Montessori also studied the traffic pattern of the rooms, arranging the furnishings and the activity area to minimize congestion and tripping. The children loved to sit on the floor, so she bought little rugs to define their work areas, which the children quickly learned to walk around. Over the years, Montessori schools extended this environmental engineering throughout their buildings and outdoor areas, designing child-sized toilets and low sinks, windows low to the ground, low shelves, and miniature hand and garden tools.

The larger educational community eventually adopted some of these ideas, particularly at the nursery and kindergarten levels. Many of the puzzles and educational devices now in general use are direct copies of Montessori's original ideas.

CHAPTER 5

Expansion of the Movement

The first Children's House received overnight attention, and thousands of visitors came to see for themselves the school in which young children of the most profound poverty and ignorance taught themselves how to read, write, do mathematics, and run their own schoolhouse with little or no adult supervision.

Their fame spread, and, consequently, all kinds of people visited the House of Children, including state ministers and their wives, with whom the children behaved graciously and beautifully without anyone urging them. Even the newspapers in Italy and abroad became excited. So the news spread until, finally also, the Queen became interested. She came to that Quarter, so ill-famed that it was considered hell's doors, to see for herself the children about whom she had heard wonders.

—Dr. Maria Montessori

A Dutch classroom in the mid-1930s situated in the small town of Laren.

Worldwide interest surged as Montessori duplicated her first school in other settings throughout Europe and then in the United States, with the same results.

Many political leaders of that time saw this as a practical way to reform the outmoded school systems of Europe and North America, as well as an approach that they hoped would lead to a more productive and law-abiding populace.

Scientists of all disciplines heralded its empirical foundation and the accelerated achievement of young children. Dr. Montessori rode a wave of enthusiastic support that should have changed the face of education far more dramatically than it has.

Dr. Montessori's prime productive period lasted from the opening of the first Children's House in 1907 through World War II (1939–1945). During this time, she continued her study of children and developed a vastly expanded curriculum and methodology for the elementary level. And she developed an intriguing vision for the secondary level.

In response to the pleas of so many earnest admirers, Dr. Montessori arranged to give her first training course for teachers in 1909. She was amazed to find that her first course attracted teachers from all over the world, who were moved to make great sacrifices to learn from her personally.

Dr. Montessori captured the interest and imagination of national leaders and scientists, mothers and teachers, labor leaders, and factory owners. As an internationally respected scientist, she had a rare credibility in a field where many others had promoted opinions, philosophies, and educational models that were not readily duplicated.

As teachers from many countries carried her ideas back to their homelands, national organizations were established. Many of these evolved independently of a continued association with Dr. Montessori and her closest circle of colleagues.

Dr. Montessori made two extended trips to the United States, in 1913 and 1915. Attentive crowds greeted her wherever she spoke. Her first book about the work in Rome was translated into English by her American sponsor, S.S. McClure, publisher of the enormously popular *McClure's Magazine*.

McClure gave the book its succinct title, *The Montessori Method*. The term stuck in the United States and abroad.

The Montessori Educational Association, whose members included Alexander Graham Bell and then-president Woodrow Wilson's daughter, supported Dr. Montessori on her U.S. tours. Dr. Montessori gave lectures at the White House and Carnegie Hall.

During her 1915 visit, she arranged for an entire class to work in a special glass schoolhouse at the Panama-Pacific International Exposition in San Francisco. The children went about their tasks under the scrutiny of thousands of visitors from around the world.

Dr. Montessori also conducted a teacher training course in California and addressed the annual conventions of both the National Education Association and the International Kindergarten Union. In 1915, the U.S. Congress introduced a bill to establish several teacher education colleges that would bring the Montessori approach to the country's public schools. Their one condition was that Montessori make her home in the United States, an offer she graciously declined, remarking that her findings could never belong to just one country but must be shared around the world.

In 1914, Professor William Heard Kilpatrick published a scathing critique of Dr. Montessori's ideas. He inaccurately accused her of being rigid and outdated in her psychological theories, and her methods began to fall out of favor in the United States. Kilpatrick, a colleague of the highly popular American educational reformer Dr. John Dewey of the University of Chicago, led many initially enthusiastic supporters back to Dewey's progressive education movement. Progressive education declined from the 1930s through the 1950s, as schools in the United States moved from a child-centered perspective to a basic skills focus.

Dr. Montessori's influence in the United States slowly ebbed from its peak in 1920, when the country had more than 1,000 Montessori schools, to the period from 1930 to the late 1950s, when only a handful of Montessori schools worked quietly without openly using her name.

DR. MONTESSORI'S LATER YEARS IN EUROPE AND INDIA

Dr. Montessori eventually moved to Barcelona, Spain, where she established an international training center and research institute.

In 1919, she began a series of teacher-training courses in London. During the next three decades, she and her colleagues refined the elementary Montessori program and opened classes for older children across Europe.

The same year, Dr. Montessori was invited to give a series of lectures on education for the young adult. These talks, later published as the "Erdkinder Essays," reflected a solid theoretical basis for her thoughts about the reform of secondary education; however, she never developed them herself. Others did pursue this path, and the first secondary schools following the Montessori approach opened in the Netherlands in the 1930s. After many years of fits and starts, Montessori secondary programs have finally begun around the world.

In 1929, Italian dictator Benito Mussolini invited Dr. Montessori to introduce her ideas throughout the Italian national school system. Mussolini's invitation was irresistible to the Italian-born, self-declared citizen of the world. In January 1930, Dr. Montessori returned to Rome to much fanfare and reestablished her teacher-training center.

It is fascinating to consider what each of the two, liberal Dr. Montessori and fascist Benito Mussolini, were thinking. He certainly sought to add Dr. Montessori's worldwide acclaim to the glories of modern Italy. We assume she believed she could quietly do her work without getting involved in politics. Ultimately, the two clashed publicly when Mussolini demanded that all students in Italy join the Fascist Youth Organization and wear a special student uniform. In 1934, Dr. Montessori was forced into exile and returned to Barcelona.

The years leading to World War II were tumultuous for Dr. Montessori, who was then in her sixties. In 1936, as the Spanish Civil War broke out across Spain, she escaped on a British cruiser sent to rescue British nationals. She traveled to the Netherlands, where she opened a new Montessori teacher education center and lab school.

As war approached, many urged her to leave Europe, and in 1938, she accepted an invitation to conduct a series of teacher training courses in India. When India entered World War II as part of the British Empire, Montessori and her son, Mario, were interned as enemy aliens. However, she was allowed to continue her work and trained more than 10,000 teachers in India and Sri Lanka over the next few years.

During this period, she wrote several of her most important works, including *The Absorbent Mind*, *Education and Peace*, and *To Educate the Human Potential*. Having spent years educating teachers to grasp the big picture of the interdependency of all life on Earth, she reflected on global conflict and humankind's ultimate place within the universe, distilling them into her Cosmic Curriculum: Lessons in Science, History, and Human Culture, which has offered generations of Montessori students a sense of wonder and inspiration.

After the war ended, Dr. Montessori returned to Europe. In her final years, she became an even more passionate advocate of peace education. She was honored with many awards and nominated for the Nobel Peace Prize in 1949, 1950, and 1951. Dr. Montessori died in 1952 at her home in the Netherlands.

Dr. Montessori was a brilliant student of child development, and the approach that evolved out of her research has stood the test of time for nearly one hundred years in Montessori schools around the world. During her lifetime, she was acknowledged as one of the world's leading educators.

Mainstream education, however, moved on, adapting only the elements of Dr. Montessori's work that fit into existing theories and methods. Ironically, the Montessori approach is not designed to be implemented as a series of piecemeal reforms. It requires a complete restructuring of the school and the teacher's role.

Modern psychologists and developmental educators increasingly agree that Montessori's ideas were ahead of their time. Only recently, however, as our understanding of child development has grown, have we rediscovered how clear and sensible her insight was.

PART THREE

Key Components of the Montessori Approach

CHAPTER 6

Montessori's Core Values and Principles

Montessori schools are designed to help each student discover and fully develop their individual talents and possibilities. Montessori educators view each child as unique, allowing them to learn optimally at their own pace and in the way that best suits their learning style. The learning materials allow for a number of strategies to teach skills, and Montessori teachers strive to be flexible and creative in addressing each student's needs.

As the world changes at increasingly rapid speeds, children must learn how to learn. Montessori education promotes independent thinking and learning, not memorization. Montessori educators lead students to ask questions and discover how to find the answers themselves. Teachers encourage children to think for themselves and actively engage with the material. Older students are encouraged to research, analyze, and come to their own conclusions.

While Montessori schools have similarities, each is unique, with variations in size, facilities, programs, and school culture. Within a school, each class may look and feel different, reflecting the teacher's interests and personalities. However, specific values that honestly follow the Montessori approach should be found in all schools.

A Montessori education addresses the whole child's development—cognitive, social, emotional, physical, and spiritual. Montessori values these areas as much as their academic success. Together, they lead to a well-balanced education.

To effectively provide these opportunities, Montessori teachers must undergo specific training and certification that addresses all aspects of a child's development and is much more comprehensive than most teacher education programs.

Taken together, a core set of values guides the daily practices of an authentic Montessori school.

INTRINSIC MOTIVATION

One of Dr. Montessori's most profound fundamental discoveries is that children are intrinsically motivated. They are driven by their internal desire to become independent and competent beings.

Montessori teachers cultivate intrinsic motivation by providing children with developmentally appropriate opportunities for meaningful work. When they are engaged, students learn naturally and master new ideas and skills. Extrinsic rewards

lead most students to become dependent on external motivation. In making independent choices and exploring concepts largely independently, Montessori children construct knowledge, their sense of individual identity, and their understanding of moral right and wrong.

Dr. Montessori saw children as far more than students. In her view, each child is a whole and complete human being, the parent of the adult they will become. Even young children share humanity's hopes, dreams, fears, emotions, and longings. This goes beyond mental health to the core of one's inner spiritual life. Montessori programs offer consciously designed experiences that cultivate the child's sense of independence, self-respect, love of peace, passion for self-chosen work done well, and the ability to respect and celebrate the individual spirit within people of all ages and the value of all life.

INDEPENDENCE AND CONFIDENCE

Montessori teachers share a conviction that success in school is directly tied to the degree to which children believe they are capable, independent human beings. Young children are shown how to pour liquids, write letters, and compute sums. Older children are shown research techniques, Internet search routines, and forms of expository writing. Montessori philosophy suggests that children develop a greater sense of confidence when they are provided the opportunity to experience a meaningful degree of independence. Independence and the resulting confidence set a pattern for a lifetime of good work habits, self-discipline, and a sense of responsibility.

Most of the time, children are drawn to work that strikes their interest. However, teachers also help them choose activities that will present new challenges and new areas of inquiry. Montessori teachers also direct students to master the basic skills of their culture.

Children learn by doing, and this requires movement, active engagement with the material, and the opportunity for spontaneous investigation. Young children touch and explore everything in their environment. They investigate, manipulate, and build up a storehouse of impressions about

the physical world around them. Children develop thinking through hands-on learning.

Montessori children freely move about and work alone or with others at will. However, their freedom always exists within carefully defined limits on the range of their behavior. Free to do anything appropriate within the ground rules of the community, children are consistently redirected, promptly and firmly, if they cross the line. Children may select an activity and work with it as long as they wish, so long as they do not disturb anyone or damage anything. When finished, they are expected to put materials back where they belong.

THE NORMALIZED CHILD

At first, a child may select one tray and then another, explore its contents, and return it to its shelf location. Gradually, however, the child lengthens the time spent exploring and discovering. Movements slow, becoming precise and disciplined. Her concentration extends, and she can maintain her focus and attention. She begins to locate the ideas embedded in the learning materials and her surrounding environments. This is the process of *normalization*.

This Montessori term causes a great deal of confusion. Normalization is a terrible choice of words. It suggests that teachers help children who are not normal become normal. This is not what Dr. Montessori meant to suggest at all.

In the process of normalization, young children, who typically have short attention spans, learn to focus their intelligence, become self-disciplined, concentrate their energies for long periods, and take tremendous satisfaction from their work. The children are learning to concentrate, work independently, and complete complex tasks.

One mother said, "In Montessori, my child looks interested, sometimes puzzled, and often completely absorbed. I think of normalization as a kind of satisfaction that he seems to take from what he calls hard work."

In his book, *Maria Montessori: Her Life and Work*, E. M. Standing described the following characteristics of normalization in the child between the ages of three and six:

- A love of order
- A love of work
- Profound spontaneous concentration
- Attachment to reality
- Love of silence and working alone
- Sublimation of the possessive instinct
- Obedience
- Independence and initiative
- Spontaneous self-discipline
- Joy
- The power to act from real choice and not just from idle curiosity

OBSERVATION: THE ROLE OF THE TEACHER

People often think of the materials that are used in Montessori as the Montessori Method. These materials are, however, the result of the Method. The Method itself is observation.

Dr. Montessori taught that the purpose of observation is to assist children's growth and development. Teachers systematically and scientifically observe children's exploratory patterns of behavior. Teachers trust that children will pursue what they need to become adults. An often-heard expression of this Montessori principle of trust is, "Follow the child." Each child will explore that which interests them.

Dr. Montessori once said to parents: "Children live in a world of their own interests. The work they do there must be respected, for though many childish activities may seem pointless to grown-ups, nature uses them for her own ends. She is building mind and character as well as bone and muscle. The greatest help you can give your children is the freedom to go about their work in their own way, for in this matter, your child knows better than you."

Older children typically talk about and identify their interests; younger children may not. To discover the interests of young children, Dr. Montessori directed teachers to observe how long a child works with or stays involved with an activity.

Learning to observe requires initiation and practice. Ordinarily, we think of observation as involving perceiving or seeing. What we see makes sense to us through a process of comparing, interpreting, and reasoning.

A. A. Milne offered the following humorous expression of observation, interpretation, and reasoning.

Winnie-the-Pooh sat down at the foot of the tree, put his head between his paws, and began to think.

First, he said to himself: "That buzzing noise means something. You don't get a buzzing noise like that; you just buzz and buzz without it meaning something. If there's a buzzing noise, somebody's making a buzzing noise, and the only reason for making a buzzing noise that I know of is because you're a bee."

Then he thought for a long time and said, "And the only reason for being a bee I know of is making honey."

And then he got up and said: "And the only reason for making honey is so I can eat it." So he began to climb the tree.

Having observed, Montessori teachers can prepare classrooms where children can find activities that allow them to fully exercise their inner needs and interests. If children are interested in the activities in the classroom, the teacher has observed accurately. Observation continues, however; children do grow, and their interests change. Observation and preparation of the classroom are perpetual.

Dr. Montessori used the title *directress* instead of teacher to underscore the very different roles played by adults in her schools. In Italian, the word implies the role of the coordinator or administrator of an office or factory. Today, many Montessori schools prefer to call their teachers *guides*.

Montessori teachers facilitate the learning process by serving as a resource to which the children can turn as they gather information, impressions, and experiences.

Montessori teachers deliberately model the behaviors and attitudes they are working to instill in their students. Because of Montessori's emphasis on character development, Montessori teachers usually are exceptionally calm, kind, warm, and polite to each child.

CHAPTER 7

The Planes of Development

Dr. Montessori noted through her research that children's needs, interests, and abilities are grouped into specific *planes of development*, or growth phases. Because each plane has certain characteristics, Dr. Montessori referred to a child's development as a series of "rebirths." She believed schools should not be divided by grades but according to children's planes of development.

Dr. Montessori's study of children led her to conclude that child development is not linear. Children do not develop in a continual progression. Instead, there are predominant years of attainment (as indicated by the rising line on the diagram on this page) followed by predominant years of refinement (indicated by the falling line) within approximately six years. However, the diagram should not be interpreted to mean that children do not attain new understandings and capabilities during periods of refinement. Instead, Dr. Montessori proposed an overall tendency for attainment during the first three years, followed by a tendency for refinement during the second three years.

Montessori educators teach in partnership with students, based on a guiding trust that each child will show us when they are ready to learn the next skill or concept. Parents expect this with their children's physical skills, such as walking or talking.

Learning to read, however, can be a different matter. Parents may expect their children to begin reading before they turn five. It would be much simpler to educate children if learning to read, write, and compute arithmetic took place according to a defined schedule. Children do, however, follow their own schedule. Despite national, state, and local performance standards and requirements for teacher accountability, these skills will come when children are empowered to follow their developmental inclinations.

A fundamental Montessori principle is to respect each child as a natural person. Respect includes expressing regard and esteem. Respect also involves honoring each child's readiness for learning. Children do not usually tell us in words when they are ready. Instead, children respond to specially prepared learning environments. Montessori teachers are trained to prepare these environments and to observe for developmental signals that indicate readiness.

THE FIRST PLANE: BIRTH TO SIX

Rapid growth and development take place during the first six years of life. From considerable dependence to independence, young children learn to feed themselves, walk, run, and ride bicycles. Infants, toddlers, and combined three-to-six-year-olds are three Montessori classroom groups.

As young children develop coordination, their concentration lengthens from several minutes to more than an hour. As this occurs, the child's movements become slower, more precise, and controlled. The child becomes more ordered or self-disciplined.

The First Three Planes of Development

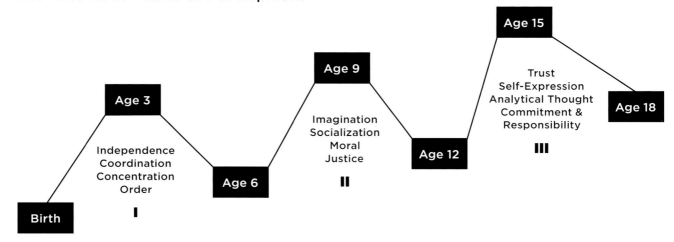

The Absorbent Mind and the Sensitive Periods

Montessori discovered two important characteristics of children before they reach the age of six. She called these the *absorbent mind* and the *sensitive periods*.

The absorbent mind refers to the idea that between birth and age three, children unconsciously absorb sensory input from the environment. This absorption forms connections between neurons in the brain. In other words, children explore, and the input they gather from the world helps form them.

This idea helps explain language acquisition. Infants become fluent without the arduous study of language required by adults. Infants hear language, observe sign language, or both, and naturally begin to talk or sign.

Dr. Montessori believed children must find a properly prepared environment to fully develop their unique human potential. In Montessori's early childhood programs, teachers provide learning environments where everything is "just right." Just as Goldilocks tested out food, chairs, and beds in the three bears' cottage and found those that were just right, food, furniture, learning activities, social relations, clothing, routines, and rituals must all be just right for each young child to develop their fullest potential.

Sensitive Periods

As we know, genetics determine a child's eventual height, hair color, and other physical characteristics. Another genetic plan determines each child's unique emotional and intellectual qualities. These qualities develop through what Dr. Montessori called the *sensitive periods*.

During the sensitive period for order, we begin to see children concentrating on completing a task following a sequence of steps.

Each sensitive period is a specific kind of compulsion that motivates young children to seek objects and relationships in their environment that will help fulfill their inner potential.

Children explore their classrooms, seeking and discovering objects and exercises that satisfy the compulsions of their sensitive periods. For example, the sensitive period of order compels children to sort and sequence objects into just the right places.

In *The Secret of Childhood*, Dr. Montessori wrote: "A child's different inner sensibilities enable him to choose from his complex environment what is suitable and necessary for his growth. They make the child sensitive to some things but leave him indifferent to others. When a particular sensitiveness is aroused in a child, he is like a light that shines on some objects but not on others, making them his whole world . . . It is during the sensitive period that he makes his [cognitive] adjustments like that of being able to adapt himself to his environment or to move about with ever-increasing ease and precision."

Each sensitive period is:

- a time of special sensibility and psychological attitudes;
- an overpowering force, interest, or impetus directing the child to particular qualities and elements in the environment;
- a period during which children center their attention on specific aspects of the environment to the exclusion of all else;
- marked by passion and commitment;
- originated from the unconscious, leading the child to conscious, creative activities;
- characterized by intense and prolonged activity that leads to persistent energy and interest, not fatigue or boredom;
- a transitory state; and
- never relived or regained, once passed.

Sensitive Periods from Birth to Age Six

Dr. Montessori identified eleven sensitive periods that occur between birth and age six. Each refers to a predisposition compelling the child to acquire specific characteristics, as described below. The ages of each sensitive period's onset and conclusion are approximate.

1. **Movement.** (Birth to one year) Random movements become coordinated and controlled: grasping, touching, turning, balancing, crawling, and walking.
2. **Language.** (Birth to six years) Use of words to communicate: a progression from babble to words to phrases to sentences, with a continuously expanding vocabulary and comprehension.
3. **Small objects.** (One to four years) A fixation on small objects and tiny details.
4. **Order.** (Two to four years) A desire for consistency and repetition and a passionate love for established routines. Children can become deeply disturbed by disorder. The environment must be carefully ordered, with a place for everything and carefully established ground rules.
5. **Music.** (Two to six years) Spontaneous interest in and development of pitch, rhythm, and melody.
6. **Grace and courtesy.** (Two to six years) Imitation of polite and considerate behavior, leading to an internalization of these qualities.
7. **Refinement of the senses.** (Two to six years) Fascination with sensorial experiences (taste, sound, touch, weight, and smell), which teaches them to observe and make increasingly refined sensorial discriminations.
8. **Writing.** (Three to four years) Fascination with reproducing letters and numbers with pencil or pen and paper. Writing tends to precede reading.
9. **Reading.** (Three to five years) Spontaneous interest in the symbolic representations of the sounds of each letter and in the formation of words.
10. **Spatial relationships.** (Four to six years) Forming cognitive impressions about relationships in space, including the layout of familiar places. Children become more able to find their way around their neighborhoods, and they are increasingly able to work with complex puzzles.
11. **Mathematics.** (Four to six years) Formation of the concepts of quantity and operations from concrete material aids.

If an environment does not contain what the child seeks, Dr. Montessori believed that children would not reach their full potential and their personalities would become permanently stunted.

These eleven sensitive periods have been observed in children from all socioeconomic backgrounds and in many cultures, including (by co-author Paul Epstein) children living in an arctic town in Sweden, the slums of Brazil, and a mountain village in Nepal.

Each plane of development has sensitive periods, though the characteristics vary by age.

THE SECOND PLANE: SIX TO TWELVE

If the first plane of development is referred to as the absorbent mind, the second plane of development is often referred to as the *reasoning mind*. The elementary child wants to know the reasons for things. This requires going out into the world to discover, understand, and find her place, including exploring the natural and social worlds through imagination.

The vast elementary curriculum includes, but is not limited to, grammar, literature, arithmetic computations, geometry properties, laboratory science techniques, ecology principles, and cultural history lessons. Elementary children prefer to learn and work together socially. They also become aware of moral values.

A seven-year-old may complain that it is not fair that someone else got a turn or received something. Later, there is a concern for social injustices. At nine or ten, the child may complain about the unfairness of homeless or hungry people or pollution.

THE THIRD PLANE: TWELVE TO EIGHTEEN

During the third plane of development, adolescents develop trust, use new forms of self-expression, exercise new ways of thinking, form relationships involving commitment and responsibilities, and form personal gender identities.

During this time, individuals may grow rapidly or gradually. Cognitive and emotional development may take longer than physical growth. The child's mental capabilities begin to mature and become more similar to those of an adult.

Young adolescents require movement and can display tremendous imagination and great humor. They also prefer conversation; a key is to provide opportunities for them to design and implement personally meaningful and socially contributing experiences.

In time, teenagers begin to understand and appreciate interdependence—relationships of integrity and reliability, with trust, honesty, and commitment. These relationships include learning to be responsible.

Dr. Montessori wrote, "There are two needs of the adolescent: for protection during the difficult physical transition, and for an understanding of the society which he or she is about to enter to play his or her part as an adult." Most adolescent programs offer academic studies involving interdisciplinary, thematic instruction with land-based learning, internships, and community service experiences.

THE FOURTH PLANE: EIGHTEEN TO TWENTY-FOUR

Even though we do not always think of the years from eighteen to twenty-four as an extension of child development, Dr. Montessori recognized this time as the fourth plane of childhood. This is the time in life when the older adolescent or young adult works to find their place in the world as a fully independent member of society. Young people usually leave the family home and move into the workplace or onto higher education while integrating their personalities, clarifying their values, and establishing their identities as mature adult citizens.

CHAPTER 8

The Prepared Environment: Curriculum and Materials

We refer to the Montessori classroom as a *prepared environment*. This name reflects the care and attention given to creating a learning environment that reinforces children's independence, creativity, imagination, and intellectual development.

A Montessori classroom is a carefully prepared learning environment.

The prepared environment is based on three principles.

- **Freedom.** Children freely choose their own work, or learning activities, based on their currently active inner sensitive period. The Montessori teacher understands that for young children, freedom is an accomplishment of the development of inner self-discipline. Adults must never do for children anything that the children can learn to do for themselves. Instead, adults must protect children's ability to choose by ensuring they can work with the selected learning materials without interruption or interference from other children.

- **Beauty.** Each learning activity is complete; everything needed is present and in good repair. Objects placed in the classroom are attractive and elegant, designed to attract the children's interest and attention.

- **Contact with nature and reality.** Classroom objects represent reality and nature. Children use real sinks and refrigerators instead of play ones. Dr. Montessori taught that a child's direct contact with nature results in understanding and appreciating order and harmony. The Montessori classroom environment is a place of life. Children learn to take care of plants, animals, and fish. Magnifying glasses, microscopes, and simple experiments allow children to observe and learn from nature.

MONTESSORI MATERIALS: THE ROAD FROM CONCRETE TO ABSTRACT THINKING

All children and most adults learn best through direct experience, investigation, and discovery. Many students do not retain or understand much of what they "learn" through memorization.

Asking a child to sit back and watch a teacher perform a process or experiment is like asking one-year-olds not to put everything into their mouths. Children need to manipulate and explore everything that catches their interest. Anyone who has lived with children understands this truth.

Dr. Montessori recognized that concrete learning apparatus makes learning much more rewarding. The Montessori learning materials stimulate children to think logically and discover.

Each age level of the Montessori curriculum includes an extensive collection of carefully defined educational materials equivalent to the chapters in a traditional textbook. Each material isolates and teaches one concept or skill at a time. In developing the materials, Dr. Montessori carefully analyzed the skills and concepts involved in each subject and noted the sequence in which children most easily master them. She also studied how children most easily grasped abstract concepts and designed each element to bring the abstract into a clear and concrete form.

In the early years, children work with tactile materials such as the pink tower, which helps them develop a sense of size and dimension. As they progress, they encounter materials such as the golden beads, which tangibly introduce mathematical concepts. These materials lay the groundwork for more abstract thinking by physically representing complex ideas.

This hands-on approach allows children to internalize concepts as they physically manipulate objects to understand their properties and relationships. This method not only aids in comprehension but also makes the learning process engaging and enjoyable.

As children move through the Montessori curriculum, they gradually shift from concrete experiences to abstract thinking, building a solid foundation for lifelong learning.

Building the pink tower

Skip counting to sixty-four using the bead chain of 4 cubed

The journey from concrete to abstract is a core element of the Montessori Method, providing children with the tools they need to understand and master complex concepts. By engaging their senses and encouraging exploration, Montessori materials help children develop critical thinking skills and a deep love of learning that will serve them throughout their educational journey and beyond.

The materials are displayed on low, open shelves easily accessible to even the youngest children. Each has a specific place on the shelves, arranged from the upper left-hand corner in sequence to the lower right, following their sequence in the curriculum. The materials are arranged from simplest to most complex and from the most concrete to the most abstract. Children can find what they need whenever they wish.

This ongoing engagement with the materials ensures that children build a deep and comprehensive understanding of the concepts they are exploring. It also encourages a sense of accomplishment and confidence as they progress from simple to more complex tasks.

Moreover, the beauty and precision of the Montessori materials invite children to explore them. These materials are carefully crafted to be aesthetically pleasing and durable, fostering a sense of respect and care in children who use them. Children are drawn to the materials for both their educational value and their visual and tactile appeal.

Combining independent exploration, self-correction, and progressive challenges creates an educational foundation supporting lifelong learning and intellectual curiosity. Montessori materials are integral to a broader educational philosophy that values independence, curiosity, and the intrinsic motivation to learn. They embody the Montessori principle that children learn best when engaging in meaningful, hands-on activities that encourage exploration and discovery.

Each material is a concrete representation of an abstract idea. Depending upon the children's ages, they will use the materials to explore and investigate ideas found in anthropology, art, astronomy, biology, botany, chemistry, earth science, geography, geology, geometry, history, language, mathematics, music, physics, and sociology.

When children choose a material, they develop independence, responsibility, and time management. They develop cognitive capabilities while investigating and using the materials to sort, arrange, build connections, and problem-solve. Educational theorists now advocate learning through direct experience, investigation, and discovery. The child must be active and engaged in constructing their knowledge.

The organization of the Montessori curriculum from early childhood through secondary programs is a spiral of integrated studies. Montessori learning

The Integrated Montessori Curriculum

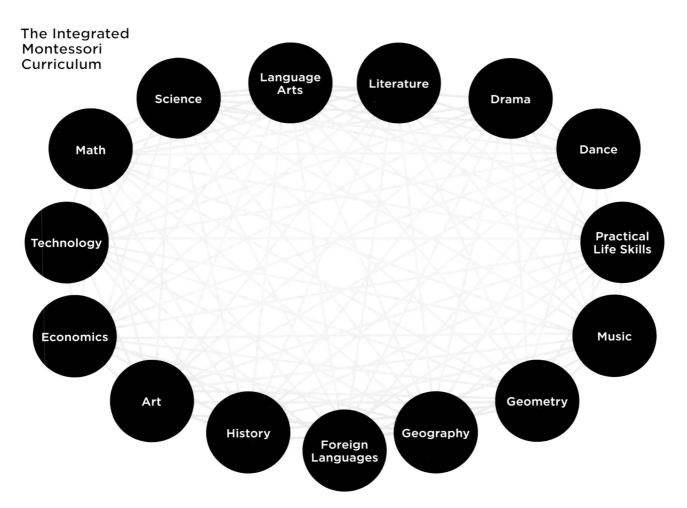

The Montessori curriculum is carefully structured and integrated to demonstrate the connections among the different subject areas. History lessons, for example, link architecture, the arts, science, and technology.

The cylinder blocks

materials offer multiple levels of challenge and can be used repeatedly at different developmental levels.

Children progress through the Montessori curriculum at their own pace, moving on to the next step in each learning area as they are ready. Initial lessons are brief introductions, after which the children repeat the exercise over many days, weeks, or months until they master it. Interest leads them to explore variations and extensions inherent within the design of the materials at many levels over the years.

THE CONTROL OF ERROR

Making mistakes is a vital part of the learning process. Discovery, investigation, and problem-solving involve making wrong turns, getting stuck, and trying again. An important part of the learning experience is learning to recognize an error and make corrections.

Montessori learning materials are designed with a built-in *control of error,* which gives children immediate feedback. Students can check whether they have done each exercise correctly.

The cylinder blocks, for example, are a set of four naturally finished rectangular blocks of wood into which ten cylindrical holes have been cut. Each hole is filled with a matching wooden cylindrical inset fitted with a little knob on the top to make it easy for a child's small hand to grasp and lift the inset out of its perfectly fitted hole. Each set of cylinders is constructed to vary in a regular sequence by either diameter, length, or both. The children remove each cylinder in turn, carefully tracing its length and circumference and the depth and circumference of each hole with one finger.

Once all ten cylinders have been removed, the children take each in turn and find the hole into which it fits perfectly, with the top of the cylinder flush with the top of the cylinder block. If they've made a mistake, the children can typically see it for themselves because all ten cylinders will not fit correctly.

The children quickly challenge themselves by attempting to see which hole is likely to fit the cylinder in their hand rather than trying to fit each into one hole after another. After a while, they will begin to do the same exercise blindfolded, relying on touch alone. Children continuously refine their work and learn more.

The Spiral of the Montessori Curriculum

- Everything is interrelated. One lesson leads to many others.
- The child moves from the concrete toward abstract understanding.
- We always work from the big picture to increasing detail.
- Every three years, major themes in the curriculum are studied again in greater depth and abstraction.

Very Abstract Work

The spiral of Montessori's integrated curriculum

Language Arts	Art	Moral	**Ages 9-12**
Geography	Music	Education	
Dance	Psychology	Observation	
Literature	Everyday	Skills	
Foreign	Living Skills	Anthropology	
Languages	Science	Nature Study	
History	Economics	Computer	
Mathematics		Skills	

Language Arts	Art	Moral	**Ages 6-9**
Geography	Music	Education	
Dance	Psychology	Observation	
Literature	Everyday	Skills	
Foreign	Living Skills	Anthropology	
Languages	Science	Nature Study	
History	Economics	Computer	
Mathematics		Skills	

Language Arts	Art	Moral	**Ages 3-6**
Geography	Music	Education	
Dance	Psychology	Observation	
Literature	Everyday	Skills	
Foreign	Living Skills	Anthropology	
Languages	Science	Nature Study	
History	Economics	Computer	
Mathematics		Skills	

Very Concrete Work

Very Complex Studies   **Very Simple Studies**   **Very Complex Studies**

PART FOUR

Practice and Implementation

CHAPTER 9

A Typical Montessori Day

It is dark at 7:45 a.m. on this midwinter morning when Jeanne Saunders pulls up to the drop-off circle at the Montessori school her three children have attended since they were two.

Imani, Justin, and Madison consider their Montessori school their second family. Madison speaks about the school with affection and conviction. Visitors often find her coming up without hesitation to greet them and offer them a cup of coffee before they start the campus tour. When people ask if she likes it in Montessori, she smiles and says, "Sure! How could anyone not love it here? Your teachers are your best friends, the work is interesting, and the other kids are my friends. You feel very close to everyone."

Madison walks her five-year-old sister, Imani, to her morning supervision room. Seven-year-old Justin goes ahead on his own.

After dropping off Imani, Madison walks into the middle school wing, where she is a seventh grader. She joins two of her friends in the commons, and they sit and talk quietly, waiting for class to start at 8:30 a.m.

Imani's morning supervision takes place in her regular classroom. After hanging up her coat, she asks Judy, the staff member in charge of her room, if she can help. Judy asks Imani to look over the breakfast table and provide any missing napkins and spoons. Imani does this, and when the table is ready, she makes herself a bowl of cereal and sits down to eat. Children and parents drift into the room occasionally; gradually, the number of children grows to about fifteen.

After eating her breakfast, Imani brings her bowl and spoon to a dishwashing table. The bowls and spoons are stacked in a bin. Later in the morning, several children will choose the dishwashing activity.

Next, Imani walks to the easel and begins to paint with Teresa, a three-year-old who has recently joined the class. They paint quietly, talking about nothing in particular.

Eventually, Imani tires of painting and cleans up. For a moment, she is tempted to walk away and leave the easel messy; instead, she carefully cleans up and puts the materials away, as she has learned from more than two years in Montessori.

At 8:30 a.m., Imani's full-day teacher and her assistant arrive, along with several more children.

Twenty-four students and two adults quietly move about the room. During the next several hours, Imani and her classmates will choose learning activities individually and in small groups. They will have a variety of lessons from their teachers. Some will be demonstrations of learning materials. Other lessons will be direct instruction on, for example, the phonetic sounds of letters or on names for numerals, geometric shapes, and geographic terms for landforms, continents, and nations.

In another part of the school, Justin and his classmates begin their lower-elementary day (for children aged six to nine) with a writing prompt: "Wisdom is . . . " As they complete the writing task, teachers meet with students to review the progress of their work plans. Soon, Justin will join a small group for an introductory lesson on using the science discovery boxes, focusing on asking investigative questions.

The middle school students start their day with a morning meeting. By sharing something that has taken place during the past twenty-four hours, students come to know one another better and build trust.

Afterward, they will break into math groups. Madison and two of her classmates will present a lesson demonstrating the predictive power of a linear equation. Following math, the students will regroup into smaller teams. Each team is completing research for multimedia presentations based on topics from their global studies.

Meanwhile, back in the early childhood classroom, Imani and one of her friends are constructing and solving a math problem: 2,346 + 1,421. This activity reflects their learning accomplishments during the past two years. Each child has used other materials to build an understanding of numbers and place values.

Today, they use a set of numeral cards to make the first addend: 2,346. The cards showing units 1 through 9 are printed in green. The cards showing the tens numerals from 10 through 90 are printed in blue. The hundreds are printed in red, and the cards showing 1,000 through 9,000 are printed in green again because they represent units of thousands.

Imani and her friend looked through the cards and found a green 6, a blue 40, a red 300, and a green 2,000. They place these numeral cards across the top of a wooden tray and carry it to the "bank," a central collection of golden bead materials. They place their tray on the floor, and they gather six unit beads.

Next, they count out four bars of ten beads, which will represent 40. This process is repeated until their tray is filled with the correct number of hundred squares and thousand cubes. They walk back to their workspace and unroll a rug on the floor. The girls place their numeral cards across the top of the rug. They place the unit beads under the green 6 card; four bars of ten beads under the blue 40 card; three squares of hundred beads under the red 300 card; and two cubes of thousand beads under the green 2,000 card. The girls then fill their empty trays with cards to form the numeral 1,421. Walking to the bank, they again select the correct quantity of bead materials and return to their work rug. They build 1,421 under the 2,346.

Children doing math with the golden beads

Children usually choose when to have a snack.

The two addends are combined in an addition process: the unit beads are combined and placed in the lower right corner of the rug. The ten bars are combined and placed to the left of the units. This process continues for the hundred squares and thousand cubes. Their movements mimic the pencil and paper process. Beginning with the units, the children count the combined quantities to determine the result of adding the two together. In this example, the result is seven unit beads. They find a green 7 card to represent this partial sum. If their addition resulted in a quantity of ten beads or more, the children would stop at the count of ten and carry the ten unit beads to the bank, where they would exchange the ten unit beads for one ten bar. This process of counting and labeling quantities is repeated for the tens, hundreds, and thousands.

Imani and her friend collected pieces of math paper and green, blue, and red pencils to complete this activity. They copy their problem on their papers: 2,346 + 1,421 = 3,767. They put their papers in their cubbies, and they return the pencils, numeral cards, bead materials, and tray to their proper places.

Finally, they roll up their work rug and return it to the rug holder. As the children proudly say, this is a "big work."

It is now almost 10 a.m., and Imani is hungry. She moves to the snack table and prepares several pieces of celery stuffed with peanut butter. She pours a cup of apple juice, using a little pitcher just the right size for her hands. When finished, Imani takes the cup to the dish-washing table and wipes the placemat. As with the breakfast dishes, dish-washing is a real-life activity; the children will wash their own dishes and learn to care for their needs. (Dishes and utensils will go through the dishwasher before the next morning.)

Cleaning up from her snack has put Imani in the mood to really clean something. She begins a table-washing activity.

Imani finds her friend Chelsea, and they talk about a puppy named Sam. They begin to laugh as their story becomes increasingly elaborate. Their teacher, Ann, acknowledges their creativity and suggests they write a story. This lesson involves a work rug, a box of wooden letters called the moveable alphabet, pencils, paper, and writing tables,

Washing a table

The moveable alphabet

which they use to compose a story. Like the earlier math work, it reflects enormous achievements in language learning. They have already learned the phonetic sounds of letters and how to blend sounds together to write and read words. This activity also reflects enormous achievements in developing focus, concentration, and self-discipline.

Throughout the morning, Imani's classmates complete learning activities that include sorting and sequencing objects, identifying names for nations, arranging geometric shapes, and exploring scientific properties.

In many ways, Imani and her classmates are responsible for caring for this child-sized environment. Older children show younger children how to use the materials. Children prepare their own snacks by cutting raw fruits and vegetables. They go to the bathroom without assistance. When something spills, they help one another clean up. They sweep, dust, and wash windows. They set tables, tie their shoes, and polish silver. Noticing that the plants need water, Imani carries the watering can from plant to plant, barely spilling a drop.

Imani's class eats lunch at 11:45 a.m. Then they go outside to play. Soon, the Spanish teacher arrives to work with small groups of students.

Throughout their day, Imani and her classmates make responsible choices regarding which learning activities to do next. Each activity engages the children in movement patterns that form a foundation for neurological development.

Young children are comparative thinkers. They learn one thing is big when something else is small; one thing is loud when something else is soft. They are problem solvers. They can group congruent objects together; other objects are arranged sequentially by one or more properties of size and color. Repeated use of the materials allows young students to build a clear inner image of, for example, place value: How big is a thousand compared with hundreds, tens, and units?

The design of the learning materials—their sizes, shapes, colors, textures, and weights—holds students' interest and attention for long periods of time. The children explore and discover differences and similarities among objects.

As these children engage in long periods of concentration with the learning materials, they develop and display self-discipline. Their movements are orderly. Children act with grace and courtesy; they are considerate and respectful toward one another. At the same time, children are energized by their discoveries and investigations. Self-discipline involves learning to channel their energies by choosing new activities.

Children test one another: "What geometric solid is this?"

In the afternoon, Imani does an art activity, listens to selections from a recording of the *Nutcracker* ballet, writes the names of shapes taken from the geometric cabinet, and completes a puzzle map of the United States.

When the day is over, Imani will have completed ten to fifteen different activities, most representing curriculum content that is quite advanced for someone who just turned five. But when her dad picks her up at 4:50 p.m., her response to the usual question of what she did that day is no different from many children: "Stuff. I did a map and, oh, I don't know." Madison and Justin will furnish similar responses, focusing instead on what might happen during the evening at home.

Children use a set of metal insets to learn how to trace around the edges of the frame and the geometric shape inset then carefully color them in with parallel strokes to develop hand-eye coordination. The design of the learning materials—size, shape, color, texture, and weight—holds the students' interest.

CHAPTER 10

Key Components of a Montessori Classroom

In some ways, a Montessori classroom is similar to a traditional classroom. But it does have some unique characteristics, from the mixed ages of students to the look and feel of the room to the role played by the teacher.

THE THREE-YEAR GROUPING

Children in a well-run, established Montessori class are typically independent and self-disciplined. One key factor that makes this possible is continuity, as each class ideally retains two-thirds of its students each year.

Every child has a unique learning style. Montessori teachers treat children as individuals, customizing lessons to fit their needs, personalities, and interests. Since Montessori allows children to progress through the curriculum at their own pace, there is no academic reason to group children strictly by grade level. In a mixed-age class, children can always find peers working at their current level.

The levels usually found in a Montessori school correspond to the following developmental stages of childhood:

- Infant (birth through eighteen months)
- Toddler (eighteen months to three years)
- Early childhood (three to six years)
- Lower elementary (six to nine years)
- Upper elementary (nine to eleven years)
- Middle school (eleven to thirteen years)
- High school (fourteen to eighteen years)

As children grow older and more capable, they assume a more significant role in helping to care for the environment and meet the needs of younger children in the class. The focus is less on the teachers and more on the entire community of children and adults, much like in a family. A child experiences courtesy and trust, two essential aspects of optimal learning conditions.

Spending two or three years in the same class allows students to develop a strong sense of community with their classmates and teachers. This age range also offers exceptionally gifted children the

Younger children tend to be drawn to older children's work.

stimulation of intellectual peers without requiring them to skip a grade, which can lead to feeling emotionally out of place.

To accommodate the needs of individual learners, Montessori classrooms include a curriculum that covers the entire span of interests and abilities, from the youngest to the most advanced students.

In these multilevel classrooms, younger children are constantly stimulated by observing the engaging work of the older students. Older students serve as tutors and role models for the younger ones. Children pick up skills (and habits) from older children as they learn to navigate each level of development.

This process benefits both the tutor and the younger child. A larger group size focuses less on the adults and encourages children to learn from one another. The older child has the opportunity to be the leader or role model, providing the opportunity to feel the responsibility of modeling.

The Montessori classroom model offers a dynamic and supportive learning community where children are encouraged to grow at their own pace, learn from one another, and develop solid and lasting relationships with their peers and teachers. This approach helps cultivate independent, confident, and well-rounded individuals.

CLASSROOMS: THE LOOK AND FEEL

Montessori classrooms are bright, warm, and inviting, filled with plants, animals, art, music, and books. They are equipped with intriguing learning materials, mathematical models, maps, charts, artifacts, and a natural science center.

Most rooms include a small classroom library. Shared materials like drawing paper, exercise notebooks, or colored pencils are collected for easy access.

The walls are free of clutter, posters, whiteboards, video screens, or displays of multiple children's artwork. Any art on the walls is framed and displayed nicely.

Ideally, each early childhood Montessori classroom has one or more single-person bathrooms with a sink and toilet. A child-sized sink and counter are in the classroom for practical life work.

Child-sized furniture is made of natural wood. Tables and chairs are light enough for young children to move around the room.

Ideally, each room has direct access to an enclosed outdoor environment or a little greenhouse for gardening.

Children work on the floor using small mats that they unroll to serve as their workspace, or they may work at a table. Materials are often displayed on a two-handed carrying tray on the shelf. Children select an exercise and take it to their work area. Many classes prepare cards with children's names and pictures to identify a rug or work placed on a table.

Montessori classrooms rarely have teacher's desks or loudspeakers. Instead, most teachers ring a small bell when they need to get children's attention.

Many rooms have adult-sized chairs for observers who come to visit. Parents, prospective families, and visiting teachers can often be found watching children work. Children tend to be so involved in their work that visitors notice the peaceful atmosphere. They frequently remark on feelings of comfort, safety, and calm.

In today's world, safety concerns lead many schools to become fortresses. We acknowledge security concerns, but ideally, schools will find ways of achieving a reasonable level of safety while ensuring that children are not denied access to an outdoor environment. Perhaps the schools of tomorrow will begin to be designed like traditional walled villas, where behind the front gate, we find beautiful gardens.

THE STRUCTURE OF THE SCHOOL DAY

In Montessori, the school day is not divided into fixed periods for each subject. Teachers call students together individually or in small groups as they are ready for lessons.

A typical day's work is divided into faculty-assigned fundamentals and self-initiated projects and research selected by the student. Students work to complete their assignments at their own pace. Teachers closely monitor their students'

progress, keeping the level of challenge high. Teacher feedback to students and parents helps students learn how to pace themselves and take personal responsibility for their studies, essential skills for later success in college and life.

We encourage students to work together collaboratively. Students share their interests and discoveries. The youngest experience the daily stimulation of their older friends and are naturally spurred on to be able to do what the big kids can do.

THE TEACHER'S ROLE

Montessori teachers do more than present a curriculum. The secret of any great teacher is helping learners open their minds and hearts and become ready to learn, where the motivation is a fundamental love of learning. As parents know their children's learning styles and temperaments, teachers, too, develop this sense of each child's uniqueness.

The teacher's role is to observe and guide rather than to instruct directly. Teachers carefully watch each child to determine when they are ready for new challenges and when they need additional support. This personalized approach ensures that each child progresses at their own pace, experiencing both success and challenge in a balanced manner.

Dr. Montessori believed that teachers should focus on children as individuals, not on the daily lesson plan. Montessori nurtures human potential, leading children to ask questions, think for themselves, explore, investigate, and discover.

LEARNING HOW TO LEARN

The Montessori approach is often described as an education for life. When we try to define what children take away from their years in Montessori, we need to expand our vision to include more than just the basic academic skills.

Montessori schools work to develop culturally literate children and nurture their fragile sparks of curiosity, creativity, and intelligence. They have a very different set of priorities than traditional schools and have little regard for mindless memorization and superficial learning.

Our goal is less to teach them facts and concepts than to help them fall in love with focusing their complete attention on something and solving its riddle. Work assigned by adults rarely leads to such enthusiasm and interest as work that children freely choose for themselves. The Montessori classroom is a learning laboratory where children can explore, discover, and select their own work.

Children become comfortable and confident in their ability to master the environment, ask questions, puzzle out the answers, and learn without the constant intervention of an adult.

I believe that every child has hidden away somewhere in his being noble capacities which may be quickened and developed if we go about it in the right way, but we shall never properly develop the higher nature of our little ones while we continue to fill their minds with the so-called basics. Mathematics will never make them loving, nor will accurate knowledge of the world's size and shape help them appreciate its beauties. Let us lead them to find their greatest pleasure in nature during the first years. Let them run in the fields, learn about animals, and observe real things. Children will educate themselves under the right conditions. They require guidance and sympathy far more than instruction.

—Helen Keller and Anne Sullivan

Students need opportunities to learn through trial, error, and discovery. They need time to practice and apply new skills and knowledge. Rather than give students the correct answers, we ask the right questions in Montessori, leading them to discover the answers themselves. We encourage students to research, analyze their findings, and come to conclusions. Montessori students are actively engaged in the learning process! They learn to not be afraid of making mistakes. Few things in life come quickly, and in school they can try again without fear of embarrassment.

Even our youngest children see others working courteously with one another. They quickly learn not to interfere with someone else's work unless asked to join. They learn to walk calmly through the room, speak politely to friends, and clean up after themselves. While working alone or with friends, they may not disturb others. Montessori schools give children a sense of belonging to a family and help them learn how to live with other human beings.

We help young children set increasingly high goals for themselves. Studies show that long-term academic success is tied directly to the degree to which students see themselves as capable and independent. Montessori excels at this. If they knew the words, even very small children would ask, "Help me learn to do it myself!"

CHAPTER 11

Infant-Toddler Programs

An ironic prejudice about education exists in almost every country: the older the students a teacher works with, the higher the pay and respect the teacher will earn. We take it for granted that a university professor holds a more prestigious position than a high school teacher, which is, in turn, considered a more sophisticated position than teaching elementary. Of course, both are far more respectable than that of a nursery-school teacher. And no one in their right mind would want to teach infants and toddlers, right?

Yet research clearly shows that the most critical period in a human being's educational and emotional development is not the years of high school and college but rather the first six years of life.

Human beings are a magical combination of at least three factors: our genetic inheritance, our biological development, and our experiences. Genetics determine our unique gifts and handicaps, predispositions, and many aspects of our interests, talents, and personalities that scientists are only beginning to understand.

However, whatever potential or predispositions we inherit from our parents will only be developed if our bodies and brains are allowed to develop properly. A child who is malnourished in the critical first six years of life or who suffers a disease or physical injury will likely develop less of their human potential than one who enjoys good health.

Like a muscle, the brain only develops through active use. This is especially true in infancy and early childhood. In the past, many people pictured a child's mind as a blank slate on which adults,

through instruction, could "fill in" the content of a good education. Another common metaphor was an empty bowl waiting to be filled with the contents of the school's curricula. Dr. Montessori demonstrated that both concepts are inaccurate.

The young child's mind is more like that of an acute observer or scientist, eager to learn, explore, try new things, and master new skills. Most importantly, with stimulation, the child's ability to concentrate, absorb, and master new ideas and skills increases, and the earlier we begin a program of intellectual, physical, sensory, and artistic education, the more dramatic the result.

The years from birth to three are a time of great sensitivity to language, spatial relationships, music, art, social graces, and so much more. If, during this period, the mind is stimulated by the child's exposure to a rich environment, the brain will develop a much more robust and lasting ability to learn and accomplish. In short, while our culture may believe otherwise, the contribution of early childhood educators is incredibly important in a child's education.

MONTESSORI FOR THE INFANT AND TODDLER YEARS

Montessori toddler classes are still relatively few and far between, and infant programs are still so uncommon that parents would be fortunate to find one in their community. The ones that do exist fill quickly.

Currently, there are few Montessori-certified infant-toddler teachers. Low student-teacher ratios make these programs more expensive to run than the classes for three- to six-year-olds. Not all schools ask parents to pay the actual cost of operation, so many schools lose money on this type of program. That said, the children with this early start will be among their very best students in the years to come.

In some cases, state regulations may prohibit schools from accepting children under age three. Similarly, in some states, operating a program at this age level may cause the school to be classified as a childcare center rather than as an educational institution.

Staff Ratio

State regulations vary, but the standard that we recommend for this age is lower than most states require—striving for a one-to-three adult-to-infant ratio or a group of nine infants to one teacher and two adult assistants. This tends to make such programs more expensive, but with the special training needed, the quality is well worth the cost. It is especially important to keep staff turnover in these programs low, as even the youngest infant tends to bond deeply with adult caregivers. Their consistency over time is vital to the program's success.

Many Montessori administrators also know that if they accept children under age three, some prospective parents will view the school as a childcare center rather than a school. Some administrators fear that might cause their entire program to lose credibility.

With the low adult-to-child ratios and the tender age of the children, parents may expect to see the teacher and assistant constantly interacting with the children. Montessori, however, encourages the development of each child's independence. In a toddler class, adults do not rush in to entertain or control the children. Instead, they quietly give lessons, redirect a child who is having difficulty, help with verbal language development, and observe and take note of the children's activities.

THE FOUR COMMON TYPES OF INFANT-TODDLER PROGRAMS

Parent-infant programs are designed to educate the parents of very young children in child development and Montessori strategies. These programs give parents an opportunity to observe their children and learn how they can best respond to their babies' needs. Usually, parent-infant programs accept children under eighteen months of age. Parents come with their children to a class held once a week. A parent-teacher discussion is often held at another time during the week. Topics include parent questions and concerns, as well as weekly issues, such as sleep, nutrition, home environment, and infant and toddler development. The staffing is commonly one certified Montessori Infant-Toddler teacher with the parents in the room.

Infant-care programs generally accept infants aged six weeks to fifteen months, which support families needing all-day care. These programs are still scarce, but they are slowly increasing. The lead teacher should be certified in Montessori infant-toddler education.

The schedule depends on the infants' needs. Each baby has a different schedule for feeding and sleeping. There should be a routine of stability and consistency; babies look for predictability.

Toddler half-day programs typically run for two or three hours a day.

We strongly recommend five-day programs rather than those offering two- or three-day options. Children, especially toddlers, need consistency and routine.

Most toddler programs begin at eighteen months or twenty-four months. Some accept toddlers as young as fifteen months. These groups commonly include children up to thirty to thirty-six months of age, at which time the child is usually ready to move into a Montessori three-to-six class.

The typical schedule in a half-day toddler class might look something like the following.

- Arrival, greeting, storing coat and bag, changing shoes, choosing work
- A work period of 1.5 to 2 hours
- Snack preparation and serving
- Group singing, finger plays, and movement to music; toddlers may or may not choose to participate
- Outdoor time: running, climbing, swinging, and exploring nature, sand, and water
- Dismissal

Staff Ratio

A group of ten to twelve toddlers would typically have a certified Montessori Infant-Toddler teacher and an assistant. Some states allow a higher adult-to-child ratio. This small class size and low adult-to-child ratio tend to make toddler programs more expensive, but once again, the quality is well worth the higher cost.

Montessori floor beds

All-day toddler programs are similar to the half-day toddler class, except that children may remain for nine or ten hours. Obviously, accommodations must be made for napping, meals, outdoor time and play, art, food preparation, and other activities.

Usually, there will be some overlap in staffing, as some staff members arrive early in the morning and leave early in the afternoon, while others arrive later and stay until the last child is picked up. Whoever remains until the day's end should be prepared to communicate with the parents about how the day has gone.

The schedule for a full-day toddler class can be more relaxed, since there is more time for work, outdoor exploration, food preparation, art activities, and an early afternoon nap.

Children move out of the toddler program into the next level when they are developmentally ready, or when they are no longer challenged and showing signs of boredom. This usually occurs when children are about two years and eight months old, but the age of transition varies.

THE INFANT CLASSROOM ENVIRONMENT

A Montessori infant classroom has an area for the youngest babies, with quilts on the floor; mirrors at floor level; mobiles to observe, bat, and grasp; balls and rolling toys to chase; and rattles and objects to hold, shake, bang, and mouth. These rooms also have low beds available for naps.

Movement is critical to brain development—it is as necessary as nutrition! Most classes for children under eighteen months will include a stair with low steps and a railing for children beginning to crawl and walk. Bars and furniture are available for children to pull themselves up. Little ones can push walking wagons before they can take steps on their own. As they begin to walk, they take along push-and-pull toys.

The infant classroom typically contains one or two low shelves with fine motor activities such as puzzles, bead-stringing, rings on posts, a pegboard with large pegs, and various containers to open and close, fill and empty.

To encourage movement, the less restrictive the clothing, the better. Clothing should not inhibit movement. Rooms are quite warm and cozy.

Practical Life and Sensorial Activities for Infants

At this level, the practical life component of the curriculum allows infants to participate in caring for themselves and eating independently.

To assist young children in gaining control of their arms and hands, we provide mobiles, rattles, and other objects. Infants like to experiment with cause and effect, such as shaking or banging a rattle to make sound.

As the pincer grasp develops (age nine to twelve months), we feed the children very small bits of food, which they can pick up and bring to their mouths.

As the child is ready for cups, we give them a small cup without a lid, about the size of a shot glass, instead of a nonspillable toddler cup. We also provide a tiny pitcher, and they begin to pour their own drinks.

When spoon-feeding a child of five to nine months of age, the child may hold one spoon and the adult another, so that the child can attempt to feed themself.

All of an infant's senses are functioning at birth and grow more acute over the first three years. Infants and toddlers are very interested in sensorial experiences. For infants, we provide rattles, bells, music, and the human voice for listening; mobiles and mirrors for visual stimulation; and varied textures for touching.

THE YOUNG TODDLER

Between the ages of fifteen and eighteen months, toddlers have a new awareness of themselves as separate, unique people. They know it is possible to act and speak, but they are often not able to do what they would like. This can be a frustrating time. Aggression, such as pushing, hitting, and biting, is common and normally outgrown as the toddler gains speech and learns other techniques for coping.

It can help tremendously for the adult to acknowledge rather than judge, saying, "I know you wanted the ball, and Stephen has it," or "You look very angry!" Toddlers do not yet have the self-control to obey consistently, so adults must supervise and offer constructive activity.

Practical Life and Sensorial Activities for Toddlers

Once the toddler is walking (at about twelve months, on average), their hands are free for work. Their interest changes to accomplishing things with their hands. They want to imitate what they see adults doing and gain independence. We mustn't expect toddlers to sit as a group for a long period.

Toddlers engage in all sorts of practical life exercises designed to help them develop eye-hand control and become more independent and confident. These include tasks such as spreading soft margarine on a cracker, using a small cheese knife to cut up a banana, polishing a mirror, using small pitchers, and much more. The young child enjoys table washing, handwashing, dishwashing, sweeping, mopping, and using tongs to transfer objects from one bowl to another.

Toddlers are learning to discriminate sounds, colors, and textures. Sensorial activities at the toddler level challenge the child to match objects by size, shape, and color or to solve simple puzzles. They especially enjoy the sensorial experiences of the outdoors, such as leaves, wind, sun, water, sand, dirt, clay, textured objects, and the smells of flowers and food.

Language, Art, and Music

The time between eighteen months and two years tends to bring an explosion into spoken language, with young children learning new words every day. First, we hear them speak using mostly nouns: "ball" instead of "please give me the ball."

As they learn to speak in phrases, toddlers begin to add the other parts of speech. Most of their vocabulary is present by their third year, and researchers estimate that by age three, most children have learned 70 percent of the vocabulary they will use as adults.

In Montessori infant-toddler environments, we provide language materials such as books, objects, and pictures for naming, but the adult must also talk and listen to the child.

Toddlers enjoy basic creative work such as cutting paper, gluing, coloring with chalk and crayons, or painting with watercolors.

Young children learn to take off and hang up their own coats.

Toddlers also learn to put on their own shoes.

We can provide music in several ways. We may sing with a large group of children or just one or two. Music need not be limited to a certain time of day. Toddlers are learning language, so they are interested in words as well as melodies. Some can sing along; some still listen. They are learning to control their movements, so they enjoy simple finger plays and movements to music.

For part of the day, we may play background music. Certain songs could signal transitions in the schedule. Toddlers may also have the opportunity to choose music to listen to on headphones. This can be very calming.

CHAPTER 12

Early Childhood Communities

Most families enter Montessori during the early childhood years, ages three to six. We call this level the Children's House.

Since the first Children's House opened in 1907, parents have been amazed to see small children cut raw fruits and vegetables, sweep and dust, carry pitchers of water, and pour liquids with barely a drop spilled.

Children usually go about their work so calmly and purposefully that it is apparent to the casual observer that they are the masters in this environment. They learn how to care for themselves, others, and the world around them.

While Montessori programs are offered at every age level, from infant through high school, most families who choose Montessori begin when their children are about two and a half to three.

A child who enters at three has two years before most schools will get serious about any foundational skills that tend to develop in Montessori. These children have the gift of time. They're allowed to explore at their own pace and be exposed to and intrigued by older children's work. We see tremendous gains, especially in areas like large and fine motor movement, vocabulary development, and the ability to voluntarily choose work and complete it with deliberation.

Children who complete the three-year cycle (ages three, four, and five) show the most significant gains. However, if a family discovers Montessori later, we encourage them to take a look. Even elementary-age children and beyond sometimes enter Montessori and do very well.

Early childhood programs have four primary goals.
1. To encourage the normal desire for independence and a high sense of self-esteem, guides provide many opportunities for self-directed learning.
2. Social and emotional learning is integrated into daily activities to help children develop the kindness, courtesy, and self-discipline that will allow them to become full members of society.
3. Critical thinking and problem-solving skills help children learn to observe, question, and explore ideas independently.
4. A balanced, comprehensive curriculum creates a spirit of joyful learning and helps children master the skills and knowledge of their society.

By adhering to these goals, Montessori guides create an environment where children can thrive academically, socially, and emotionally, preparing them for a lifetime of learning and success.

Montessori guides closely monitor their students' progress, keeping the level of challenge high.

Because they usually work with children for three years, guides get to know their students' strengths and challenges, interests, and anxieties exceptionally well. Montessori guides often use children's interests to enrich the curriculum and provide alternative avenues for accomplishment and success.

LESSONS IN PRACTICAL LIFE SKILLS

Sweeping with a child-sized broom

Loading the class dishwasher

Learning how to transfer liquids with a ladle or spoon

Learning how to wash hands correctly

Washing a table

Washing dishes

Learning to tie a bow with one of the dressing frames

Students work with the dressing frames to master the skills that classically challenge them as they take their first steps toward independence: buttoning clothes, working on zippers, tying shoelaces, and so on.

Polishing shoes

Washing windows

Flower arranging

Face washing

A vital aspect of practical life lessons is developing children's ability to control their bodies and move carefully and gracefully around the room. They walk along a line on the floor, heel to toe, carefully balancing while carrying small flags, cups, or Montessori materials.

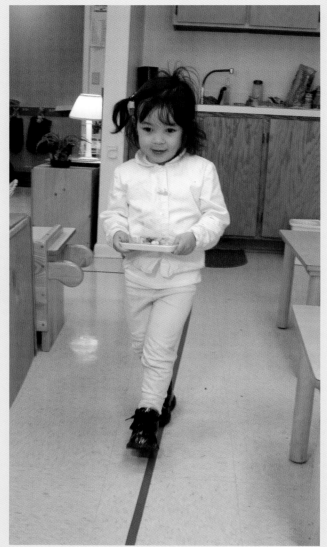

Walking on the line

Children learn to wash small polishing cloths and napkins. When the cloths are dry, students learn to iron and fold them using a special low-temperature children's iron.

Children learn practical life skills and fine motor skills by learning how to sew.

Learning how to use everyday tools

Children learn to care for the small plants and animals raised in or outside the classroom.

These lessons help them develop an inner sense of order, a greater sense of independence, and a higher ability to concentrate and follow a complex sequence of steps.

Montessori schools encourage children to develop control of their fine- and gross-motor movements. At this age level, programs will typically include dance, balance and coordination exercises, and loosely structured cardiovascular exercise, as well as the vigorous free play that is typical on any playground.

GRACE, COURTESY, AND AWARENESS

Montessori students learn practical lessons in everyday courtesy and respect, such as how to greet someone, enter a room, offer an apology, and ask if they can join an activity. Kindness and courtesy are vital practical life skills. Even the youngest child is treated with dignity and respect by teachers and classmates.

Over the years, students learn to accept more responsibility and handle themselves in various situations. Learning to live and work together with others in a peaceful and caring community is perhaps the most critical life skill that our students master.

The silence game helps children develop a much higher level of self-discipline and a greater awareness of the sounds around us. In this group activity, the teacher rings a small bell or hangs up a sign that reads: Silence. Children stop where they are, close their eyes, and try to remain perfectly still. Children wait to hear the teacher whisper their names. Then they silently rise and join the teacher.

The silence game

Conflict Resolution: The Peace Process

Two children who disagree may leave the group to solve their problem. When classmates or the teacher observe an ongoing disagreement, somebody might bring them a token, such as a talking stick or a peace rose, with a reminder to solve their problem peacefully. Montessori teaches a process for nonviolent conflict resolution. Children can retreat to a special place in the classroom to calm themselves or resolve hurt feelings. This might be a corner with cushions or a little table where the children can talk quietly.

In the following example, Eleanor is frustrated with her classmate, Lisa. At the peace table, Eleanor places her hand on the table, indicating that she wants to have her say without interruption. She places her other hand on her heart, suggesting that she is speaking the truth from her heart. She looks Lisa in the eye and proceeds to state how she feels and why, saying, "Lisa, I feel very angry because you didn't let me play with you and Lily!" Eleanor says what she would like to happen to resolve the conflict: "And I don't want you to do that ever again if you want to be my friend!" Once she has stated her case and opened the door for further discussion, she withdraws her hand and gives Lisa a chance to respond.

Lisa proceeds in the same way. She places her hands on the table and her heart, looks Eleanor in the eye, and responds, "Eleanor, I'm unhappy that you're angry. I did not mean to hurt your feelings.

However, Lily is a good friend of mine, and only two participants can play the game we played. Nobody else could have joined us if I had played it with you. So, you see, it's just one of those things. I want to remain your friend."

They continue the dialogue until they reach an agreement, even if they disagree. They talk without yelling, screaming, or blaming. They want to solve the problem.

Students learn that disturbances must be solved honestly and with goodwill to maintain a harmonious and cooperative atmosphere in the community.

In Montessori, children are taught nonviolent conflict resolution from an early age.

SENSORIAL EXERCISES

Children interact with the physical world through their senses. Many exercises, especially at the early childhood level, are designed to draw their attention to the sensory properties of objects within the environment: size, shape, color, texture, weight, smell, and sound. Gradually, children learn to pay attention, seeing small details in the things around them. They begin to observe and appreciate their environment, which is vital in helping them discover how to learn.

At first, children may be asked to sort a prepared series of objects that vary by only one aspect, such as height, length, or width. Other exercises challenge them to find identical pairs or focus on very different physical properties, such as aroma, taste, weight, shades of color, temperature, or sound. The following examples are just a sampling of materials used at this level.

The pink tower, or tower of cubes, is a graduated series of ten wooden cubes. Children carefully carry the tower, cube by cube, to the rug that defines their work area.

Children get a strong impression of size and weight as they manipulate the cubes and carry them across the room. In their work area, children look for the largest cube and begin to build the tower, one cube at a time. Once it is built, children carefully take it down and either begin again or return the cubes, one by one, to their proper place on the shelf.

Puzzles help children learn to manipulate objects and assemble a complex whole from several parts. They also introduce a tremendous range of concepts and vocabulary, from geometric shapes to the countries of the world and the parts of a flower.

Sorting

The pink tower

Working with a puzzle map

The red rods help children discover the regular progression of length.

The geometry cabinet

One child challenges another to identify the geometric solid while blindfolded.

The geometry cabinet is a set of plane geometric figures. Six drawers are fitted with several wooden-framed insets with a geometric form. Children are introduced to a broad array of complex figures, from familiar circles, squares, and rectangles to the right scalene triangle to the decagon and from the ellipse to the curvilinear triangle and the quatrefoil.

In addition to removing and replacing the pieces in their frames, children sequence some shapes by size and classify other shapes by type. They also learn to match them against printed cards representing the same figures in increasing degrees of abstraction. Gradually, children learn the names of each geometric shape. Later, they label them with preprinted name cards and eventually prepare their own cards from scratch.

Children learn the names of wooden forms representing solid geometric figures, such as spheres, cubes, rectangular prisms, square-based and broad pyramids, triangular pyramids, ovoids, ellipsoids, and cones. Children quickly begin to look for geometric forms in their environment. They also discover the relationship between the two-dimensional figures and the solid forms: a circle is related to a sphere, a square to a cube, and so on.

Touch and Temperature

Children wear blindfolds to add a level of challenge as they sort or construct with sensory materials. The mystery bag is a cloth bag or box with a hole for students to touch and manipulate objects inside. One activity is to place familiar things in the bag and challenge one another to identify them by touch alone.

Sandpaper tablets are wooden tablets covered with several grades of sandpaper. The challenge is identifying pairs with the same degree of roughness, working by touch alone. An extension uses a collection of pairs of cloth swatches cut from many different materials, each with their own textures. Again, children wear blindfolds to find the pairs by touch.

Two tools help students learn to sense relative temperature. First is the thermic jars, a set of six little metal containers. Two are filled with hot water, two with tepid water, and two with cold water. Children touch and order the matching pairs from hottest to coldest.

The thermometric tablets are pairs of identically sized objects made from materials such as wood, stone, and metal, which feel different at room temperature. The challenge is to match them by temperature and learn vocabulary such as hot, warmer, warmest, cool, cooler, and so on.

Other materials help students develop their baric sense, or ability to distinguish among objects by weight.

Sound

The sound cylinders teach children to listen attentively. Each set of six hollow wooden cylinders appears identical except for the color of its cap. Inside each set, six different substances (such as sand, dry rice, or dried peas) create distinct sounds when the cylinder is shaken. Children arrange the cylinders into two sets according to the color of their caps and attempt to match the identical pairs by sound alone. Later, they learn to grade them from the softest to the loudest sound.

The Montessori bells extend a child's ability to distinguish musical pitch. First, children learn to strike the bells with a small mallet to produce a clear note and damp them with a little felt-covered rod. Then the teacher sets out two or three pairs of bells from the two sets. Children match the pairs that produce identical notes. When they can do this easily, additional pairs are added until they can match the entire set. A more difficult exercise challenges children to grade the bells of just one set by pitch, from the lowest to the highest notes. Children often learn to play and compose little melodies as they become more familiar with the bells.

The sound cylinders

The Montessori bells

READING, COMPOSITION, AND LITERATURE

Another unusual result of the Montessori approach is that young children often can write, or encode, language by spelling out phonetic words one sound at a time, weeks or months before they can read, or decode printed words, comfortably.

Montessori teaches basic skills phonetically, encouraging children to compose their own stories using the moveable alphabet. Reading skills usually develop so smoothly in Montessori classrooms that students tend to suddenly explode into reading.

The sandpaper letters are a set of prepared wooden tablets on which each letter is printed in white sandpaper. Typically, beginning at age two or three, Montessori children are introduced to a few letters at a time until they have mastered the entire alphabet. They trace each letter as it would be written, using two fingers of their dominant hand. As children trace the letter's shape, they receive three distinct impressions: they see its shape, feel its shape, and hear the teacher pronounce its sound.

Many parents find it curious that Montessori children are not taught the names of letters. Instead, they learn the sounds we pronounce as we phonetically sound out words one letter at a time. Children call letters by their sounds: *buh*, *cuh*, or *aah*. This eliminates one of the most unnecessary and confusing steps in learning to read: "The letter *A* stands for apple. The sound it makes is *aah*."

Teachers lead children through a range of early reading exercises designed to help them recognize the beginnings of short phonetic words and later the ending and middle sounds. An example would be a basket containing *c*, *b*, and *f*. The basket includes small, inexpensive models of things beginning with these letters. This one might contain little plastic objects representing a cat, a cap, a can, a bug, a bag, a bat, a flag, a frog, and a fan. In another exercise, we substitute cards with pictures for the small objects.

The sandpaper letters

Tracing letters in the sand tray

Learning the alphabet by tracing the sandpaper letters

Once children have begun to recognize several letters and their sounds, they are introduced to the moveable alphabet, a large box with compartments containing plastic letters, organized much like an old-fashioned printer's box of metal type. Children compose words by selecting an object or a picture and then laying out the word one letter at a time.

Unsurprisingly, as young children begin to compose words, phrases, sentences, and stories, their spelling can sometimes get creative. Montessori teachers deliberately avoid correcting children's spelling during these years, building confidence in the ability to sound out words rather than risk a shutdown from frequent correction.

Composing words with the moveable alphabet continues for several years, gradually moving from three-letter words to four- and five-letter words with consonant blends (*fl*, *tr*, *st*), double vowels (*oo*, *ee*), silent *e*'s, and so on.

As children begin to write, various activities help them develop the fine eye-hand control needed for handwriting. They use metal insets to trace and shade geometric shapes and practice writing on small chalkboards.

Building words with the moveable alphabet

Beginning to compose sentences with the moveable alphabet

Learning more advanced spelling rules, such as silent e, with the moveable alphabet

Reading and Vocabulary

Learning to read should be as painless and straightforward as learning to speak. There is typically a quick jump from reading and writing single words to sentences and stories. For some children, this happens when they are four; others when they are five or six. A few read earlier or later. As with every other developmental milestone, it is useless to fret. Younger children are surrounded by older children who can read, and the most intriguing things to do in the classroom depend on one's ability to read. This creates a natural interest and desire to catch up to the "big kids" and join the ranks of readers. As soon as children show interest, no matter how young they are, we begin to teach them how to read. When they are ready, children pull it all together and can read and write independently.

Cards with the names of familiar objects are found in most kindergartens. However, in Montessori, children take this a bit further, learning and labeling a bewildering array of geometric shapes, leaf forms, the parts of flowers, countries of the world, land and water forms, and much more. Montessori children are known for their incredible vocabularies. Where else would you find four-year-olds who can identify an isosceles triangle, rectangular prism, the stamen of a flower, or the continent of Asia on a map?

An early reading exercise is a set of cards with single-word verb commands. Two or three children pick a card, read it, and perform the command: hop, smile, yawn, sleep, clap, sit, stand, wave, eat, drink, and so on. Later card sets use complete sentences such as, "Bring me the smallest cube from the pink tower," or "Waddle across the room like a duck."

Older children use command cards to suggest specific challenges in every curriculum area. In geography, a command card might challenge children to look at the atlas to find the location of the largest inland lake on Earth.

MONTESSORI MATH

The concrete Montessori math materials may be Dr. Montessori's best-known and most imitated elements. These hands-on learning materials make abstract concepts concrete. The Montessori approach offers a clear, logical strategy for helping students understand and develop a sound foundation in mathematics and geometry.

They proceed through several levels, beginning with the most basic math concepts and, presented in the most concrete representation, up through the advanced concepts of secondary mathematics, represented in increasing levels of abstraction, until the student grasps them conceptually. The examples that follow are just a small sampling of these materials.

Counting, Numbers, and Quantities

The red and blue rods provide an introduction to mathematics. These rods are painted in alternating patterns of red and blue to distinguish their length in one-decimeter segments. The first rod, painted red, is one decimeter long. The second is two decimeters long, divided into red and blue segments. This continues through all ten rods.

Dr. Montessori found that young children find it difficult to grasp the concept of numbers by counting separate objects. While they can learn to count by rote, reciting the sequence of numbers from one to ten, most cannot easily grasp the difference between one quantity and another when looking at more than three or four objects.

Children arrange the rods from largest to smallest. Then they count each alternating colored segment. Children begin to understand the nature of addition and the concept that two numbers can add up to another number. Using this series of segmented rods of increasing length allows children to visualize the concept of number and quantity.

The spindle boxes provide a structured way to understand the next concept of number and quantity. Two wooden boxes are divided into ten compartments labeled zero through nine. In a separate box or basket are forty-five wooden spindles used for counting. Children count the correct number of spindles in each compartment.

The red and blue rods

The spindle boxes

When children are ready to tackle the task of associating numeral cards and counters, or objects to count, they begin by arranging a set of numeral cards in order. Then they count out the appropriate number of counters, placing them in parallel rows. Even numbers end with an even number of counters; odd numbers only have one.

Comparing the rows introduces the concept of odd and even numbers. A later series of numeral cards helps children learn to read numerals up to 9,999. The cards introduce the concept of the hierarchy of decimal quantities and how we borrow and exchange from the next column in mathematical operations.

The numeral cards and counters

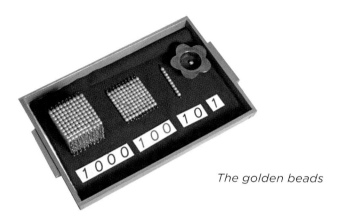

The golden beads

Children learn to recognize and write numbers by tracing the sandpaper number cards.

The bank game

An Introduction to the Decimal System

Young children commonly find it difficult to understand or operate with quantities larger than twenty. They cannot grasp the value of one hundred, one thousand, or one million, much less the idea that one thousand is equal to ten hundreds or one hundred tens.

Montessori overcame this obstacle by developing concrete, tangible materials that not only represent values but are equal in scale, representing each value of the decimal system. Units are represented by single beads. Ten unit beads strung together represent ten. Hundreds are squares made up of ten ten-unit bars; and thousands are cubes made up of ten hundred-unit squares. Because the corresponding values are constructed from smaller values, they are to scale in weight and size.

Even very young children can build and work with large numbers. From this foundation, all of the operations in mathematics, such as the addition of quantities into the thousands, become clear and concrete, allowing the child to form a clear picture of how the process works.

Often, two children work together to construct and solve a mathematical problem. Using sets of numeral cards, each collects a quantity for addition by deciding how many units, tens, hundreds, and thousands will be in his or her addend. The cards follow a color code that continues into the millions.

As the children construct their number, they decide how many units they want in their number and find the corresponding cards that represent that quantity.

Next, they go to the bank, or central collection of golden beads, and gather the number of unit beads, tens, hundreds, and thousands that correspond with their numeral cards. Students become familiar with place value and the skills of naming numerals, while also developing a deeper understanding of the value of thousands, hundreds, tens, and units.

After that, students combine, or add, the two addends. Beginning with the units, they count the combined quantities to find the result of adding the two together. If the result is nine or lower, they simply find the large numeral card that represents the answer. If the quantity is ten or greater, they stop at the count of ten and exchange the beads for the next highest quantity.

Children use the golden beads to explore the equivalencies of the decimal system.

They also learn to add multiple-digit numbers, using columns to trade groups of ten units. Once they understand how to add with the golden beads, students begin to multiply, subtract, and divide.

Concrete and Abstract Quantities

To help children begin to grasp the idea of quantities from one through nine, Dr. Montessori prepared the short bead stair, a set of colored glass beads in which each quantity is represented by the appropriate number of individual beads wired together as a bar with a specific color. A single red bead represents the number one, two green beads represent two, three pink beads stand for three, and so on, up through the ten golden beads that represent a unit of ten. Children work with the short bead stair for many years, using the material to add and subtract, exchange, borrow, explore multiples, and many other arithmetic processes.

Teens boards help students understand how numbers larger than ten are constructed and written. Eleven is one ten and a unit of one, twelve is a ten bar and a two-bead bar, and so on. The similar tens boards teach children to build and write numbers greater than nineteen to create numbers in the twenties, thirties, and beyond.

The short bead stair

The teens boards

The hundred board is divided into a grid of one hundred squares, on which children find the correct number tile.

Skip counting to one hundred using the bead chain of ten

Memorization board for addition facts

A geography area in a primary class

GEOGRAPHY, HISTORY, AND INTERNATIONAL CULTURE

We are all members of the human family. Our roots lie in the distant past, and history is the story of our shared heritage. With a strong sense of history, we can begin to know who we are as individuals today. Our goal is to develop a global perspective, and studying history and world cultures forms the cornerstone of the Montessori curriculum.

Montessori teaches history and world cultures starting at age three. International studies continue at every age level. Children learn to prepare and enjoy dishes from all over the world. They learn traditional folk songs and dances and explore folk crafts. In language arts, they read traditional folk tales, research, and prepare reports about the countries they study. Units of study often culminate in marvelous international holidays and festivals that serve as the high points of the school year.

Puzzle maps are an important element in the early study of geography. Each represents a map of the world, a continent, or the states or provinces of an individual country.

Two special globes introduce physical geography. The first teaches how land areas and water are represented on a globe. The second introduces the seven continents, each in a distinct color. Children learn the names and locations of each continent. The color code used on the continent globe is carried through in the puzzle map of the world and early work in continent studies.

A Montessori birthday celebration introduces the relationship between Earth and the Sun. Students learn that a year is how long it takes for the Earth to circle the Sun once. We place a candle on the floor and invite the child to carry a globe around the Sun once for every year of their life. After each circuit, we describe the child at that age and show photos. Children hear the story of their lives, year by year, from birth to the present day.

Land and water forms are three-dimensional models that represent basic geographic features. This is also a pouring exercise, as children add water to create a higher level of sensory impression. Here, they explore the idea that an island is a body of land surrounded by water, while a lake is a body of water surrounded by land.

Children learn to name each form, match the model with a photo of an actual lake or island, place the correctly printed label underneath each form, and then prepare their own labels. Then they learn about the largest lakes or islands in the world and research facts about specific places.

The first set of these includes such geographic forms as isthmuses, peninsulas, capes, bays, and straits. Advanced exercises introduce more complex geographic features, such as mountains, mountain ranges, volcanoes, archipelagos, foothills, cliffs, mesas, prairies, river valleys, and river deltas.

The land and water globe and the continents globe

The land and water forms

A presentation of the first puzzle map

A Montessori birthday celebration

HANDS-ON SCIENCE

The Montessori approach to science cultivates children's fascination with the universe and helps them develop a lifelong interest in observing nature and learning about the world. Children are encouraged to observe, analyze, measure, classify, experiment, and predict and to do so with a sense of eager curiosity and wonder.

With encouragement and a solid foundation, even very young children are ready and anxious to investigate their world, to wonder at the interdependence of living things, to explore the ways in which the physical universe works, and to project how it all may have come to be.

In a typical early childhood Montessori class, children learn to care for plants and learn the names of breeds of dogs and species of birds, flowers, trees, and so on. Classrooms often have a terrarium, an aquarium, and an outdoor garden. Students learn plant parts and the external body parts of familiar animals. In physical science, they work on magnetism, light, color mixing, sound, and more.

Working in the garden

THE ARTS

Art is not a separate area of the Montessori curriculum; it is an integral component. Throughout the day, even the youngest students are surrounded by beautiful materials and activities that Dr. Montessori developed for each developmental level. From the smooth, simple elegance of the geometric solids to the ever-increasing complexities of drawing using the metal insets, Montessori uses all of a child's senses to promote an awareness and appreciation of the beauty in all things, animate and inanimate.

In the early years, children are free to spend quiet moments in a special art corner of their classroom, painting, drawing, or working with crafts. Some schools employ an art specialist, and many schools expand on their art programs through special after-school workshops.

CHAPTER 13

The Elementary Level

In the elementary years, from ages six to twelve, children refine their cognitive, gross, and motor skills while developing their own unique personalities.

The curriculum in these years, made up of three core elements, is engaging and sophisticated. The first crucial part is the great lessons. These captivating stories, experiences, and research projects explain how the world came to be: the development of life on Earth; humanity's history; and the evolution of our language, writing, mathematics, and technology. The great lessons spark imagination, giving children a cosmic perspective of Earth and humanity's place in the universe.

The passage to the second level of education (age six to twelve) is the passage from the sensorial, material level to the abstract . . . Before age seven, the child focuses on a sensorial exploration and classification of the relationships among concrete objects—not exploration on the intellectual plane. The three- to seven-year-old generally is content to know what something is, along with a simplistic explanation of its function. The older child is oriented toward intellectual discovery and investigation.

In the second period, the child needs wider boundaries for his social experiences. He needs to establish social relationships in a larger society, and the traditional schools . . . can no longer be sufficient for him. He feels the closed environment is a constraint, which is why children of this age may no longer go to school enthusiastically. He prefers to catch frogs or play with his friends without adult supervision.

It is at age seven that one can note the beginning of an orientation toward the judgment of acts as right or wrong, fair or unfair . . . This preoccupation belongs to a very special interior sensitivity—the conscience . . .

These three characteristics—the child's felt need to escape the closed environment, the passage of the mind to the abstract, and the birth in him of a moral sense—serve as the basis for a scheme at the elementary level.

—Dr. Maria Montessori

The second period focuses on mastering fundamental skills and basic core knowledge. These might be considered core academic subjects, including mathematics, science, technology, literature, geography, history, economics, and anthropology. It also covers conventional curriculum basics, such as math facts, spelling lessons, the study of vocabulary, grammar, sentence analysis, creative and expository writing, and research skills.

Lastly, the Montessori curriculum encourages student-initiated, individually chosen research on topics that capture their attention. Students do a great deal of independent reading and library research. Rather than using textbooks, elementary students gather information, prepare reports, teach their peers, and assemble portfolios. As they progress, their presentations and research reports become more sophisticated and complex.

The secret of good teaching is to regard the child's intelligence as a fertile field in which seeds may be sown to grow under the heat of flaming imagination. Our aim is not only to make the child understand, and still less to force him to memorize, but so to touch his imagination as to enthuse him to his innermost core. We do not want complacent pupils but eager ones. We seek to sow life in the child rather than theories, to help him in his growth, mental and emotional as well as physical, and for that, we must offer grand and lofty ideas to the human mind. If the idea of the universe is presented to the child in the right way, it will do more for him than just arouse his interest; it will create in him admiration and wonder, a feeling loftier than any interest and more satisfying.

—**Dr. Maria Montessori**

In a dark room, with a flashing strobe, this gifted elementary guide gave a lesson about the big bang that captured the students' imagination. The expression on their faces says it all.

THE GREAT LESSONS

As children enter the second plane of development, they are able to think about people from other parts of the world, examine similarities and differences in different cultures, and recognize common characteristics of what it means to be human. They are also able to understand time as a measured and regular continuum.

Each of the six years of the elementary Montessori program begins with a representation of the five great lessons, which provide an overview of the Montessori elementary curriculum. The great lessons include the following.

- The Story of the Universe
- The Coming of Life
- The Story of Humanity
- The Story of Language
- The Story of Numbers

The great lessons introduce big concepts in a way that ignites students' interest and imagination. The way students interpret these stories and what they take away from them will change as they grow. More importantly, these stories and the curriculum are meant to teach students not only about the world, cultures, peoples, and times beyond their own but also to help them develop a deep appreciation for the world around them.

The sense of appreciation is fundamental to children's understanding of themselves in the world, as well as to the Montessori worldview, in which humans are a part and piece of a vast, interconnected world.

For example, the Montessori curriculum explores the history of the universe, life on Earth, and how we humans are the product of a series of successful mutations. Everything that happened during those billions of years before the earliest life had

to happen to spark the first living organism. Then, those organisms had to survive and reproduce, changing over time into all the living organisms that have existed, most of which no longer exist. As humans, we have to understand that we, too, are the product of a series of successful mutations along the phylogenic path. It was, however, because of our ancestors that we are able to live as we do today.

The fourth and fifth great lessons tell the story of language and numbers, which are human constructs. They explain why humans developed language and numbers as they evolved from nomadic travelers to civilizations and early towns and villages.

Furthermore, all technology, algorithms, poetry, and so on are the result of discoveries from many years ago. We owe much to those who came before us.

Discussions about the topics introduced in the great lessons continue throughout the elementary years.

The timeline of life on Earth

LANGUAGE ARTS

The elementary language arts program stresses composition and creative writing and the idea that language, both spoken and written, is a vital component of communication. The ability to articulate thoughts is a key goal of the curriculum. As technology has changed throughout the years, new tools have been built for communication.

As children grow, Montessori increasingly focuses on research and writing skills. This overlaps with the other areas of the curriculum from which students draw topics of interest. Gathering information from encyclopedias and library reference books, students learn to prepare reports. They learn to use primary and secondary resources to support their own original thoughts.

Creative writing is equally important, as students are encouraged to write and share their stories, plays, poetry, and class newspapers.

One key to the elementary language arts curriculum is the quality of the material children read. Instead of basal readers, we use first-rate children's books and fascinating works on science, history, geography, and the arts. Many elementary classes follow the Junior Great Books program or other programs that introduce classic literature, with formal literary studies continuing every year through graduation. Literature is connected with all areas of the curriculum, with students reading stories and plays about cultures and historical periods they are studying. In this way, Montessori cultivates a deep love for the world of books.

Students write continuously, initially emphasizing the enjoyment of the writing process rather than the strict use of correct grammar and spelling. This helps students develop their ability to compose, get words from their minds into another form for others, and build stamina to write in-depth and at length.

Elementary children are usually quite interested in words and sentences. They like to parse and analyze. In this way, they clarify their understanding of the structure of language that they absorbed unconsciously in early childhood classes. While they study the theory of grammar, spelling, and sentence analysis, they also expand their knowledge of written language.

We begin teaching children the functions of grammar and sentences as they are learning to put words together to express themselves. Dr. Montessori created a set of symbols to represent each part of speech, which helps children learn them quickly during a time in their lives when it is a delight rather than a chore. For example, the

Diagramming a simple sentence

symbol for a noun is a large black triangle. The symbol for a verb is a large red circle (implying a ball or movement, since verbs describe action), and the symbol for an adverb is a smaller orange circle, showing that it is related to the verb.

Over time, students systematically learn formal grammar, spelling, and sentence analysis. One underappreciated aspect of Montessori language materials is the way in which they explore the analytic side of language and prepare students not only for advanced work in grammar but also for other analytics processes such as geometry, arithmetic, and science. Language materials explore such concepts as the role words play in sentences and how we know which ones are nouns, verbs, predicates, or subjects.

Learning phonograms

The grammar symbols (parts of speech)

MATHEMATICS

Elementary students rarely have the ability to think abstractly. Anything not connected to their own concrete experience tends to be confusing. Mathematics is inherently abstract. Montessori uses concrete, hands-on materials to help children develop an inner picture of mathematics that will last a lifetime.

Dr. Montessori often used the analogy of preparing a smooth runway for an airplane. Once the plane has gained enough speed, it can travel quickly in any direction. The challenge is to provide a safe, smooth environment for the airplane to transition from being stationary on the ground to soaring through the air.

The Montessori math materials offer a prepared environment, or runway, in which children can begin to think and operate mathematically. Naturally, children can't depend on the materials

forever. The purpose of the curriculum is to make the abstract concrete, so children can close their eyes and visualize mathematical processes at work. Step by step, the materials become less concrete and more symbolic.

Students use concrete materials to perform an operation, such as carrying or borrowing, and then, as they demonstrate understanding, they transition to abstract operations using algorithms, which they can perform in their heads. Students do not simply memorize an algorithm and the correct operation. They understand what the algorithm represents, as well as the relationships between values.

The elementary curriculum introduces the fundamentals of algebra, geometry, logic, and statistics, along with the principles of advanced arithmetic. It includes the basics students need to progress to the next levels of algebra, geometry, trigonometry, and calculus.

Simple addition with the stamp game

Tools to Move from Concrete to Abstract Thinking

The golden beads and colored bead bars concretely represent quantities as three-dimensional objects. The materials are tokens, symbolic counters identical in size and differing only in color and label that represent different quantities. The stamp game is a box containing little wooden tiles. (Originally, Dr. Montessori used paper squares that looked like postage stamps.) Some are green and labeled *1* to show that they are units. Blue stamps are labeled *10*. Red stamps represent one hundred. The green set is labeled *1,000*.

Children use the stamps in the same way they used the golden beads, laying out quantities using the tokens to add, subtract, multiply, and divide. Children usually write their work on paper at this level and use the stamps to help them visualize the process.

Montessori introduces children to pre-algebraic concepts at the early childhood level through concrete materials such as the squares and cubes of the numbers one through ten. Students can build binomials, trinomials, quadrinomials, and larger polynomials, varying the values for the component parts. This is all designed to help students grasp pre-algebraic concepts at an abstract level.

The binomial and trinomial cubes are two of the most fascinating materials in the Montessori curriculum. At one level, they are a complex puzzle that challenges students to rebuild a set of cubes and rectangular prisms into a larger cube. Color coding helps children detect the pattern. The material is also an exercise in algebra and geometry, representing in concrete form the cube of a binomial $(a + b)$ and a trinomial $(a + b + c)$, where $a = 2$ centimeters, $b = 3$ cm, and $c = 4$ cm.

The bead frame is a higher level of abstraction than the stamp game.

The short division board offers another pathway to abstraction.

Long division with the racks and tube materials

Long multiplication with the checkerboard

The cubing material

The binomial cube

Later on, students will use the cubing material in a more advanced exploration of the nature of polynomials and the relationships between their component parts.

As children become more comfortable with the golden beads, they begin to ask whether anything is smaller than the unit. The fraction skittles introduce the concepts of a quarter, a half, and a whole. The fraction circles take this concept further. This set of ten metal frames has ten circles. One is left intact. One is divided into two parts, and the rest into thirds, fourths, and fifths through tenths. Children learn the terminology and how to write fractions as figures. They explore the concepts of equivalence (2/4 = 1/2) and basic operations with fractions (1/2 + 2/4 = 1).

By this stage, children record their work on paper, although many won't be able to solve the same problems without the visual aid of the Montessori materials. Most young children under the age of seven or eight find it difficult, if not impossible, to grasp abstract quantities and what happens when we add, subtract, multiply, or divide.

The bead cabinet holds the squares and cubes of the numbers one through ten.

The fractions materials

Working on the square of a binomial in three dimensions

HISTORY, GEOGRAPHY, AND ECONOMICS

The study of history, geography, and other cultural areas is meant to help students recognize not only the interdependence in all of humanity but also the common threads among cultures and peoples throughout history.

The cultural area of the Montessori curriculum integrates all of the subjects, weaving facts together to make them come alive. Children learn to look at a culture, past or present, from many perspectives. They study the environment, the climate, the look of the land, the food people would have eaten, how shelters and homes were built, and how things were transported.

These studies come alive through a host of hands-on projects and activities. A group of students interested in Greek mythology may build a model of ancient Athens or make and decorate replicas of Greek vases to illustrate a story. Alternatively, they might prepare a diorama of a mythological theme or write and produce a play for the class.

Practical economics is another vital curricular element. Students learn how to compare prices against value, compute costs, maintain checkbooks, operate small school stores, along with exploring the stock market. These topics introduce entrepreneurship and finance, crucial components of independence that will develop further in secondary programs. Dr. Montessori suggested that being financially independent and knowledgeable is a critical contributor to independence in young adulthood.

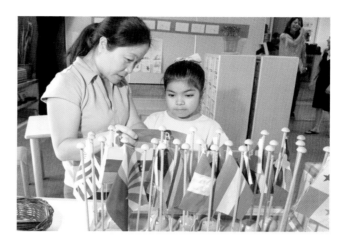

Students study the flags of the world.

Researching ancient civilizations

Learning to tell time

Elementary lab science

STUDENT-INITIATED RESEARCH AND EXPLORATION

Montessori inspires students to pursue their own interests within and beyond the classroom curriculum. Students studying an ancient civilization may research a particular component that interests them, such as the diet of early Aboriginal people or the health care practices of early Mesopotamia, which they may present to their classmates as part of their unit study.

Students also undertake independent research, such as the history of Shetland ponies, either alone or with a small group. Students who research what they care about often do so with pleasure and excitement rather than a sense of obligation.

The elementary years are the primary sensitive period for acquiring cultural literacy. Older children want to know why things are as they are in the world. They are oriented toward intellectual investigation and discovery. During these years students might become inspired to research specific or obscure topics.

COMMUNITY AND COMMUNITY SERVICE

Montessori schools are generally small, close-knit communities. Everyone knows everyone else. Children become close with their teachers and classmates. They grow up and study together for many years. Parents are usually very involved at the elementary level. They may come in to teach lessons, take small groups out into the community for field trips, and help with celebrations and performances.

Field trips are an integral part of elementary programs. Students visit destinations such as planetariums, art galleries, zoos, museums, colleges, hospitals, veterinary clinics, wildlife refuges, libraries, laboratories, factories, businesses, and centers of government. Children typically suggest and organize their field trips for the class or small groups. By initiating a proposal, developing the plan, and making and carrying out all arrangements, they gain a great sense of individual power and dignity.

These students have begun on their path of independence from the adults in their lives. One goal is that students start to realize that they do not need to be dependent on adults and are, in fact, capable, independent beings.

Music class

Students sometimes ride bikes in the community.

Children also learn social skills, courtesy, conflict resolution, and ethical behavior. This provides a platform for them to work together, acknowledge one another's contributions, and develop a sense of justice and moral reasoning. Students actively explore questions of social justice, human rights, aid to people in need, and global peacebuilding.

As the curriculum begins to focus on the world outside of their own direct experience, students begin working with groups outside of their classroom. Classes often recycle and prepare compost. They may clear stream beds, plant wildflowers, and participate in erosion control programs. Most will raise funds for charities or to support a child through an overseas aid organization.

Students write letters to lawmakers and decision-makers about social and environmental issues. They also tend to talk about the issues of the day with their friends and families.

They may work with younger students or participate in service projects outside of the school. Students develop a sense of civic responsibility and the feeling of being capable contributors to the community.

Students study the work of local, state, and federal governments and begin to follow current events. During election years, they might meet candidates and discuss the issues of the day. Politics, or the activities associated with governing a body of people, are more visible and polarizing than at any other time in recent history. The goal of a well-run Montessori elementary program is not to influence and certainly not push a specific agenda but to introduce different types of governments and political affiliations, with the emphasis on participation, as students determine their own paths based on their own feelings about what is right or wrong, fair or unfair, just or unjust.

Through these and other efforts, we introduce Montessori children to moral questions in personal relationships and encourage the awakening of their social conscience. They engage in a gradual process of self-discovery and start to ask larger questions: What do I do well? What do I stand for? What is the purpose of my life?

More importantly, a Montessori elementary program aims to equip students with the skills they need to actively define their path in life. This includes making decisions to change paths when necessary and striving to lead balanced and successful lives, defined by their own standards of success rather than those of others.

This social sense often presents itself as students becoming invested in social or environmental issues. One by-product of fostering independence and self-confidence is that students will have the desire to make change and believe that they are, in fact, agents for change.

ELEMENTARY MONTESSORI TEACHERS

The comprehensive elementary curriculum requires teachers to have a broad and thorough education of their own. With lessons that range from the history of mathematics to the physics of flight, mineralogy, chemistry, algebra, geometry, and literature, to name just a few, Montessori educators need to be generalists.

Rather than providing the right answers, teachers ask the right questions. Students are encouraged to do their own research, analyze what they have found, and come to their own conclusions.

Guides attempt to make each lesson as enjoyable as possible, using higher-order thinking questions to connect the lesson to students' interests. For example, they might say, "Today, I've brought in a live lobster, and I have room for eight of you who are interested in learning about crustaceans and how they live. If you are interested, you may join me." In the lesson, they may ask students to explore their knowledge of lobsters, such as why they have an exoskeleton and what makes them arthropods. Guides invite students to voluntarily join a lesson, knowing that on some days, no children will participate.

INTRINSIC MOTIVATION

Children may find some things difficult or particularly easy. They can recognize their best learning style and learn to pursue not only those things that they find interesting or that come easily, but also how to accomplish things that they would rather avoid.

Montessori does not just prepare children to make a living; it prepares them to make a balanced life for themselves. This requires a nurturing environment. We argue that if children are stopped by self-doubt, afraid of looking foolish or fearful of failure, then the grade or approval of parents and teachers becomes an end in itself, rather than what is really important. We want children to discover the joy of exploring ideas and figuring things out.

The true challenge of education is to keep the spark of human intelligence and curiosity alive. A vital part of being human is recognizing that the world is vast and fascinating. We should never be afraid to ask questions, wonder why things are the way they are, or explore how things might be.

Human beings have always learned as much from their mistakes as their successes. However, when parents and teachers look at young children's early creative writing and find creative phonetic spelling or sloppy handwriting, they may focus on what children did incorrectly rather than what they did right. When parents are disappointed with a child's early efforts, they subtly communicate that their expectations have not been met. Their children then learn to protect themselves by quietly pretending that they do not care or by choosing not to share information with their parents when they can avoid it. We need to help children discover their own unique talents and capacity to create and learn.

Essentially, we want students to do their best and explore their interests and passions out of intrinsic motivation, not for the sake of praise or to avoid criticism. Montessori students tend to carry this value into the world, doing their best because it is the right thing to do, not for external validation or to avoid negative consequences.

PHYSICAL EDUCATION, HEALTH, AND WELLNESS

The Montessori approach to health and fitness helps children to understand and appreciate how our bodies work and how to care for and feed a healthy human body. Students typically study

nutrition, hygiene, first aid, response to illness and injury, stress management, and peacefulness and mindfulness.

Daily exercise is an essential element of a life-long personal health program. Students typically explore many alternatives. They may practice daily stretching and exercises for balance and flexibility. Some programs introduce yoga, tai chi, or aerobic dance. Cardiovascular exercise can come from a wide range of enjoyable activities, such as walking, jogging, biking, rowing, calisthenics, using stationary exercise equipment, swimming, golf, or tennis. They may enjoy vigorous games and organized sports, long hikes, horseback riding, gymnastics, or dance.

Social and emotional health are equally important and deserve the same amount of time and reverence. Montessori programs, at all levels, aim to help students learn to manage their own emotions, conflicts, and mental health.

PRACTICAL LIFE SKILLS

Elementary children are ready to take on a much higher level of challenge and responsibility. The classroom community is run almost entirely by the students. They keep the room in order, care for classroom animals, tend to the plants and perhaps a small garden, set up for lunch, organize special events, and generally move about the school much more independently. They are responsible in many cases for conflict resolution and solving the challenges between individuals or for the whole class. They often write and produce their own plays, designing costumes and scenery with little help from adults.

Children learn how to cook and bake, use a washing machine, iron a shirt, arrange flowers, fix a bicycle, tie knots, use hand tools, plan a party, comparison shop, train a dog, dress appropriately for any occasion, write thank-you letters, prepare for a long hike, pack a suitcase or backpack, babysit, learn self-defense, and observe everyday rules of etiquette. Many students serve on school safety patrols or assist in preschool classrooms.

ASSESSMENT: HOMEWORK, TESTS, AND GRADES

Many parents have heard that Montessori schools do not believe in homework, grades, and tests. Furthermore, many people associate these three elements of traditional education as the only forms of assessment. This is a misunderstanding.

Montessori education at all levels is based on assessment and uses a variety of assessment methods, including student work, interactions with materials and other students, observation, and more formal traditional assessment. What makes Montessori different is that it does not use "high-stakes" assessment.

Many students find sewing or knitting to be a relaxing brain break from challenging work. This young child is learning the first steps in sewing.

One way Montessori teachers assess students is to have them teach a lesson or give a presentation to the class.

Homework

Most Montessori schools assign little to no homework. When homework is given, students engage in meaningful, interesting assignments that expand on their classroom studies. When we challenge or invite children to do assignments at home, the work provides an opportunity to practice and reinforce skills introduced in class. As children grow, completing assignments independently helps develop self-discipline.

Homework should never become a battleground between adults and children. As parents and teachers, our goal is to help children learn to get organized, budget time, and follow through until the work is completed. Ideally, home assignments will give parents and children a pleasant opportunity to work together on projects, providing both with a sense of accomplishment while enriching and extending the curriculum.

For example, elementary classes may send home a packet of at-home challenges. The children have an entire week, including the weekend, to complete them. The following Monday, teachers review with the children what worked, what they enjoyed, and what they found difficult or unappealing.

Depending on the child's level, Montessori at-home assignments might be organized into three groups.

- Experiences might include reading a book, going to a play, planning a meeting, or interviewing a grandparent. Students exercise skills and may engage other members of the family. The student should be actively involved in deciding what the deliverable is.
- Another type of assignment is to learn something new, likely associated with what the student is working on at school. Successful completion would allow the student to present to or teach classmates.
- Submitting a completed product may also be part of an experience. Products may include plays, essays, stories, experiments, or models. If students are reading a book, they may create a play of a particular scene or even write a piece from the perspective of a character.

Teachers typically create opportunities to choose from several assignments. Sometimes, teachers prepare individually negotiated weekly assignments with each student. This is based on the observed phenomenon that whenever students voluntarily decide to learn something, they are passionate enough to engage with tasks beyond the classroom.

Follow-Up Work, Work Plans, and Work Journals

After new concepts or materials are introduced, students may complete follow-up work to demonstrate understanding. Ideally, the includes the opportunity for choice. If children are studying the relationships of lines, they could create a poster or a book, write and record definitions, find examples in their environment, or suggest another way of demonstrating that they understand.

A challenge and opportunity for Montessori guides is to provide options that let children meet their learning style and demonstrate mastery in a way that appeals to their strengths and gifts.

Montessori children usually work with a written study plan for the day or week. It lists the basic tasks they need to complete while allowing them to decide how long to spend on each and what order they would like to follow. Beyond these assignments, children explore topics that capture their interest and imagination.

Many schools use work journals, in which students record how they spend their time and track their work. This tool introduces expectations, making choices, and time management. The student can go back and evaluate how they spent their time, reflecting on how it aligned with what they had hoped to accomplish. These tools prepare students for successful transition into middle school programs, where they will have more independence and higher expectations.

Montessori gives students the opportunity to choose a large degree of what they investigate and learn, as well as the ability to set their own schedule during class time. Individually tailored expectations don't mean that students can do whatever they want academically. They cannot elect whether or not to learn to read. Montessori students must live within a cultural context, including the mastery of skills and knowledge that we consider basic.

Tests and Formal Assessment

Montessori children usually don't think of our assessment techniques as tests so much as challenges. Most teachers give informal individual oral exams or invite children to demonstrate what they have learned by either teaching a lesson to another child or providing a formal presentation. The children also take and prepare their own written tests to administer to their friends. Rather than being graded using a standard letter-grade scheme, students are usually working toward mastery.

Reporting Student Progress

Because Montessori believes in individually paced academic progress and encourages children to explore their interests, we don't assign grades or rank students according to achievement. Parents, students, and guides give and receive feedback in several different ways.

Student self-evaluations. Elementary students prepare a monthly self-evaluation of their previous month's work. Then they meet with teachers, who review it and add comments and observations. Students also prepare self-evaluations of the past three months' work: what they accomplished, what they most enjoyed, what they found most challenging, and what they would like to learn in the months ahead.

Portfolios of student work. Teachers and students review completed work two or three times a year and make selections for their portfolios. The portfolios are compiled into a digital or physical collection to be shared with parents and kept as a keepsake of the year's work.

Conferences. Parents, students, and teachers hold family conferences two or three times a year to review portfolios and self-evaluations and discuss progress.

Narrative progress reports. Once or twice a year, Montessori teachers prepare written narrative evaluations of students' work, social development, and mastery of fundamental skills.

A Montessori View of Standardized Testing

While Montessori students tend to score very well on standardized tests, Montessori educators argue that standardized testing is inaccurate, misleading, and stressful for children. Educators have several concerns, including how well a given test captures a sense of someone's actual skills and knowledge. Because Montessori education uses different language, standardized tests may not adequately capture a student's ability, yielding inaccurate results that can be misleading to parents, teachers, and school administrators.

Any given testing session can be profoundly affected by the student's emotional state, attitude, and health. To a large degree, what they really demonstrate is how well a student knows how to take this kind of test. Montessori educators further argue that formal tests are unnecessary, since any good teacher who works with the same children for three years and carefully observes their work knows far more about students' progress than any paper-and-pencil test can reveal.

The ultimate problem with standardized tests in many countries is that they depend very much on whether a school is consciously teaching students the content that will be measured and whether it needs to be understood in other schools. Tests are helpful when seen as a simple feedback loop, giving both parents and the school a general sense of how students are progressing.

Although standardized tests may not offer a terribly accurate measure of a child's basic skills and knowledge, in our culture, test-taking skills are just another practical life lesson that children need to master. Administrators should work with parents to clarify the role test-taking plays, what the tests measure, and how the results will be used.

CHAPTER 14

Middle and High Schools

Montessori middle schools serve as a bridge between the nurturing environment of elementary education and the increased responsibilities of high school. These programs are designed around the developmental needs of early adolescents, ages twelve to fifteen, who are characterized by their quest for independence, social identity, and intellectual engagement.

THE PSYCHOLOGY OF THE ADOLESCENT

Puberty is a period of physical, cognitive, emotional, and social makeover. Childhood concludes, and in a few short years, an adolescent becomes an adult. Teenagers are often described as out-of-control risk-takers and sensory seekers. They can be defiant and rebellious, and they challenge limits and push boundaries. Alternatively, teenagers are described as lazy, moody, and egocentric.

The Montessori view of adolescence differs remarkably from these stereotypes. Dr. Montessori described the adolescent as a "social newborn" who embarks on a noble journey, a developmental quest to become an adult. Adolescents seek answers to questions about identity and purpose: *Who am I? Why am I here? Do I live for myself, or is there something more to do?* Dr. Montessori recognized the adolescent's desire to contribute to others. Education must, she argued, nurture, support, and teach adolescents to find themselves, contribute, and make a difference.

Some areas of growth happen before others. New brain cells are created, new connections are made, and older connections are pruned away.

This process begins in the limbic system, in the emotional center of the brain. Controlling, processing, and expressing emotions may be difficult during the growth period of ages ten to thirteen. Many parents describe their young adolescents as impulsive and often explosive.

The redesign of the brain's architecture also includes the prefrontal cortex, where decision-making, self-control, and understanding consequences occur. Full development of this part of the brain may not be complete until age thirty-one or thirty-two. Until then, adolescents and even young adults utilize the amygdala to make decisions. The amygdala processes sensory information, determines if we are in danger, and then responds. We either fight, flee, or freeze. When a teenager acts impulsively, we see evidence of the amygdala at work.

Another part of the brain that undergoes restructuring controls responses to pleasure. This part of the brain releases dopamine, which both reinforces and motivates behavior. Adolescents seek excitement and thrills, which release more dopamine.

As the brain eliminates unneeded neural connections and strengthens other

Discussions in secondary Montessori classes are ongoing.

neural connections, things work more efficiently. Adolescents can process information and respond more quickly than younger children. Everything feels big and urgent.

At the same time, young adolescents are rebalancing their bodies. Tremendous physical growth is happening in their bones and muscles. Coordination is a challenge as bones lengthen before muscles develop. Some young people are physically awkward as their body's center of balance is thrown off. Parents often describe their teenagers as out of control when they throw books on a table or slam a cupboard door. And they may be out of control until they learn to manage their new adultlike bodies.

As the body and brain grow, adolescents develop their capacity to think about thinking. They learn to reason hypothetically, predict and plan ahead, understand analogies, and construct metaphors. However, because of the brain's reorganizational process, concentration is often difficult, especially during the younger adolescent years. They are easily distracted.

Young adolescents are also concerned (and sometimes overly preoccupied) with justice and fairness. Injustice (as they define it) bothers them. They have a strong desire to help others. In the process, they develop their social abilities and learn about social roles.

Adults have learned to behave more or less appropriately for each role. For example, adult

spouses know how to share and discuss certain information that is usually inappropriate to share with employers or employees. Adults can also quickly adopt different social roles. Each morning at home, an individual may be a spouse and a parent. Then, at work, they are an employer or employee. Later, depending upon situations, the individual may be a daughter or a son, a sibling, or a friend. Other roles include renters, homeowners, customers, coaches, investors, worshippers, gym members, and more.

Adolescents are learning about social roles, and learning to behave appropriately for each role requires practice. Mistakes happen often, and adolescents often behave inappropriately during social situations. Friends are exceedingly important for most adolescents. They provide an emotional safety net as young people venture out of childhood and try out new ideas, behaviors, and social roles.

Friends make up an adolescent's social community, and Montessori teachers support and guide adolescents as they develop their social skills and community. Knowing how to live interdependently is one such skill. In adult terms, interdependence involves being trustworthy. Interdependence requires being able to give and keep your word, to be trusted and depended on. Effective communication skills, shared inquiry, problem definitions, and multiple approaches to generating and adopting solutions all rest on reliability.

Adolescents' chief approach for developing interpersonal reliability is through self-expression. Talking is one way adolescents learn to adopt social roles and develop integrity. Friends talk and then repeat what was said. They may even text or email the content of their talk. Some of the information is confidential, and a trusted friend will keep their word and not share it with others.

Adolescent Developmental Characteristics

12 YEARS	18 YEARS
Needs social validation	Increased self-reliance
Needs to present ideas and talents to peer groups	Needs to present talents and ideas to the world at large
Sensitive and impressionistic; quick to accept	Capable of individual articulation and analysis
Enjoys creative work, but easily distracted; concentration is difficult	Enjoys creative and analytical work; can focus for lengthy periods
Intolerant of hypocrisy and failures in others	Tolerant of failures and shortfalls in others and self
Concerned with social justice; often critical of others	Concerned with individual justice on a larger, international scale; more accepting of other perspectives and values
Impulsively articulates ideas, feelings, and thoughts	More reflective; shows care for others when articulating ideas, feelings, and thoughts
Identifies self with place (home, school)	Can bring identity into the outside world
Tries on ideas and opinions; may accept ideas and opinions to please	Considers, questions, and applies ideas and opinions
Blindly loyal	Practically loyal
Boundless energy; welcomes physical, hands-on activities	Boundless energy; welcomes hands-on activities

Adapted from Gena Engelfried's *"When Is It Time to Grow Up? Contrasting the Needs and Characteristics of the Twelve- to Fifteen-Year-Old and the Fifteen- to Eighteen-Year-Old."*

Secondary students often go out into the community or travel for field studies.

SECONDARY PROGRAMS AND CURRICULUM

Montessori high school programs support and develop students' emerging abilities of higher metacognition, concerns for social justice on a global scale, and determination to take on more responsibilities. One principal described a group of students who came to him with a plan to establish a student-led theater/dance performance troupe. Although the principal was required to assign a teacher as an adviser, the students took charge and identified and solved problems on their own, leaving the adviser with little to do.

Students use some Montessori materials for review or advanced study purposes. But the prepared environment for adolescents is not a classroom. It is the entire world. Adolescents develop age-appropriate independence skills when they originate and justify their innovative solutions to real-world problems.

Dr. Montessori first proposed her ideas for secondary programs in a series of letters to parents in Amsterdam in the late 1920s. These parents wanted to extend the Montessori experience for their children beyond the elementary school years. The first Montessori secondary school, Amsterdam's Montessori Lyceum, opened in 1930 with 157 students; today, the school enrolls more than 1,500 students.

At first, Dr. Montessori envisioned expanding her model of elementary education into the middle and high school years. But in 1932 she believed that Montessori-educated twelve-year-old children had already reached the educational level of fifteen-year-olds. So Dr. Montessori proposed a set of secondary education reforms.

Erdkinder

Young adolescents may think of themselves as all grown up, but there are few real-world places for them to go. Community playgrounds are made for younger children, and shopping malls are designed for adult buyers.

Dr. Montessori understood the significance of a place designed for young adolescents, and she considered a farm to be an ideal setting for the reform of secondary education. She called her program *Erdkinder*, a German word for "children of the land."

The Erdkinder reforms offered a radically different kind of school. Dr. Montessori believed that the farm environment provided opportunities for holistic development. Young adolescents were not there to become farmers. By living independent of their families for a few years in a small rural community, young people could engage in challenging intellectual and physical activities while learning practical habits, values, and skills needed to assume the role of an adult. She envisioned students working side by side with adults on a working farm, including selling farm products at local markets. Students would, under adult supervision, manage a hostel or hotel for visiting parents. Farm management and store economics form the basis for meaningful academic studies. The Erdkinder would have a "museum of machinery" where students could assemble, use, and repair their own farm equipment.

Very few programs adhere to Dr. Montessori's original intent in offering students a residential farm experience. Most modern programs are located in urban or suburban settings. Instead of living on a farm, students may participate in Erdkinder weeks or land-based activities in a rural setting.

UNIQUE CHARACTERISTICS OF MONTESSORI SECONDARY PROGRAMS

While a universal model for Montessori secondary programs does not exist, most blend several essential components: a vibrant adolescent decision-making community; challenging academic courses that may incorporate inquiry- and project-based learning; a variety of athletic, art, music, dance, and drama activities; entrepreneurial business experiences; internships; community service; and opportunities for domestic and international travel. In addition, some programs blend Montessori principles with other educational practices, such as the International Baccalaureate's middle years and diploma programs.

Students are often engaged in projects around the school campus.

Graduating seniors

A Student-Centered Community

The adolescent community is central to Montessori secondary schools. Community building, social responsibility, and ethical development cultivate not just knowledgeable students but also compassionate and engaged citizens. Mixed ages are still a component of secondary programs. Students may be grouped into two- or three-year age groups.

It is within the adolescent community that each student experiences a process Dr. Montessori called *valorization*, or self-worth. This happens when a student successfully overcomes challenges and completes responsibilities. When adolescents feel capable and self-sufficient, they experience valorization. They feel joyful and optimistic. They develop a love of work, study, and achievement. They experience life's value and purpose, and they become confident in their abilities to succeed through their own efforts and in collaboration with others.

Students practice adultlike responsibilities when they serve as leaders in student community meetings. They are responsible contributors as they discuss and resolve issues and propose and implement new activities. Each student participates in the planning and operation of school programs.

Rigorous Academic Courses

Students engage in a sequence of mathematics, history, science, humanities, the arts, physical education, and foreign languages that may initially look familiar.

Instead of segregating academic subjects, Montessori programs integrate disciplines, reflecting the interconnectedness of knowledge and life. Teachers guide students beyond traditional subject boundaries and lead them to make interdisciplinary connections. Projects often combine science, mathematics, literature, and social studies, mirroring real-world complexities and fostering an international perspective. Students are encouraged to take charge of their education, set goals, and manage their time.

Schedules are built around extended blocks of time, allowing for hands-on activities and collaborative projects. This approach fosters deeper understanding and retention as students engage with a variety of interdisciplinary, thematic units of study. Each study stimulates thinking, problem-solving, creativity, communication, project planning, and project implementation.

The following example was developed and implemented by co-author Paul Epstein in collaboration with secondary teachers at the Brookview Montessori School and the Rochester Montessori School in Minnesota.

The thematic units of study in this two-year middle school course integrate history, geography, science, and English literature. Students in grades seven and eight work and study together. Each theme lasts eight weeks.

Each thematic study is organized around a central concept, which provides focus and enables

intercultural understanding and connections among various traditions and information disciplines.

Each thematic study is also guided by a large essential question. An essential question is open-ended and debatable. It transcends culture and time because today's answers may be different the next time the question is asked.

The A Year

	First Quarter	Second Quarter	Third Quarter	Fourth Quarter
Eight-Week Thematic Unit	I-Machine	Planet Earth: So, who's in charge?	Howdy, Partner	E-Citizen
Central Concept	Change	Culture	Systems	Responsibility
Essential Question	Do I need technology, or does technology need me?	How am I responsible for planet Earth?	Are fairness and justice merely ideals?	Am I a consumer or an originator of innovation?

The B Year

	First Quarter	Second Quarter	Third Quarter	Fourth Quarter
Eight-Week Thematic Unit	Home Page	Me, Inc.	Money, Money, Money!	Innovators and Heroes
Central Concept	Place	Identity	Life	Innovation
Essential Question	Who am I in an interdependent world?	How am I known?	What is wealth, and what is its cost?	How can I make a difference?

Students plan or discuss topics in study groups.

The student-centered learning activities in a unit of study are organized and presented as study guides. Each guide is like a college course syllabus, presenting students with learning objectives, a schedule of lessons, and a schedule of assignments. In keeping with Montessori practice, a study guide offers students several choices about what to work on and when their assignments are due.

Teachers adjust learning activities according to individual needs, interests, and learning pace. Many studies are designed for inquiry, or discovery-based learning, instead of teacher-directed lectures. Students work individually or in small groups on projects that include authentic, performance-based instruction. Seminar discussions include analyzing text, developing thinking skills, and practicing listening skills.

Learning activities include opportunities for self-expression in a variety of forms as students construct personal meaning about their studies and themselves. Instructional methods include projects, lectures, case studies, fieldwork, seminar discussions, debates, artistic media, journaling, theater productions, educational games, field trips, essay writing, interviews, poster presentations, video productions, panel discussions, portfolio presentations, TED Talks, timelines, online quests, and more.

Faculty mentors instruct and support students as whole persons who develop knowledge, skills, self-esteem, responsibility, compassion, and citizenship.

Meaningful real-life and real-world problems engage students in developing applications and solutions that involve higher-order thinking and research skills. For example, co-author Paul Epstein's middle school math students determined how much beef one million people living on Mars for a year would need to consume to stay alive!

Clearly stated academic objectives provide structure for a wide variety of self-evaluations and formative and summative project assessments. Epstein's students once designed imaginary planets with made-up land, water, and life forms. Students explained and justified their designs by applying their knowledge of the effects of gravitational and geological forces on planets, as well as the principles of evolution.

Students develop a broad worldview, recognizing their role as global citizens. They explore topics such as the philosophical considerations of relationships between people and nature, human history and the role of individual contributions, scientific causality, and understanding mathematics and applying data to big, real-world questions.

The curriculum is rigorous, with opportunities for in-depth research, scientific experimentation, and creative expression. Students may examine climate and ecological issues by considering various economic and political perspectives, moral values, and philosophical connections between the natural world and cultural history. Students may also participate in weekly internship programs as they work side-by-side with adults in a variety of professions.

Student-Run Businesses

Secondary students work together to operate economically viable businesses. Dr. Montessori believed living and working on a farm would develop skills of responsibility through the immediate effects of their work. As one student put it, "I learned it doesn't matter how I feel. The farm never sleeps."

Developing an entrepreneurial mindset is a key educational goal. Students learn to plan budgets, apply principles of accounting, prepare and present financial statements (income, expenses, profits, loss), propose and make data-based business decisions, produce products, design and implement marketing, develop customer service and hospitality skills, track sales, and analyze production costs. Students also develop leadership and management skills as they lead work teams, plan and run business meetings, and more.

Student-run morning coffee shop

One school's culinary arts program

Student-run businesses include coffee shops, school lunch programs, bakeries, bee colonies for honey production, and gardens and chicken houses for the sale of produce and eggs. Other examples are bicycle repair shops, manufacturing Montessori classroom materials, school yearbook production, and making and selling jewelry, clothing, and scented soaps.

Profits from the business may be reinvested to sustain and grow the business or applied to student travel experiences.

Community Service

Service activities at this level include volunteering at homes for seniors or in community gardens, tutoring younger students, serving food at local shelters, animal care, river and other ecological clean-ups, collecting and distributing books, volunteering to assist at races, and much more.

Through service activities, young people develop project management skills, teamwork, commitment, self-esteem, and personal integrity. Contributing to making life better for others is an expression of noble work and engages an adolescent in the process of valorization.

Travel Study Programs

Travel opportunities allow students to plan budgets and itineraries. In one example, students experienced Spanish language and cultural immersion on a study in Costa Rica. Their purpose involved ecological and biological field research experiences in a rainforest and a coastal beach. They stayed with local families, attended classes on sustainability issues and preservation projects, and participated in community service activities with younger children in a local Montessori school.

Travel experiences engage students with many real-life challenges, including how to finance a trip. Students plan and implement fundraisers and use profits from their entrepreneurial businesses.

A high school research trip to Spain

PART FIVE

Beyond the Classroom

CHAPTER 15

Montessori at Home

Let's explore how you can nurture your children's love for learning and independence, sparking their curiosity and excitement.

The principles of Montessori begin early. During the first few months of life, young children learn how to roll over, creep, and sit. Crawling follows at about eight months, and most children will begin to "toddle" around twelve months. During the child's first year, it is critical to provide an environment for movement. We avoid containing children in playpens, cribs, walkers, jumpers, and child carriers except when necessary for travel or short periods. Instead, we provide time for the young child to be on a quilt on the floor, where they can move freely.

We recommend a tiny table and a chair with arms instead of a high chair as the child begins to eat solid foods at five or six months of age. For diaper changing, since it is so easy for children to fall from changing tables, we recommend a pad on the floor in the bathroom instead.

THE DRIVE FOR INDEPENDENCE AND SELF-CONFIDENCE

As children grow, they seek independence. They want to feel capable and respected. Driven by their intense desire to become competent, children may become frustrated and have tantrums. Your role as a parent is to empower. By treating your children with respect and encouraging them to try new skills, you foster their independence. However, if you find joy in doing things that your children can do for themselves, you may unintentionally hinder their independence and delay development of their self-esteem. A child who feels respected and competent will develop greater emotional well-being than one who is simply loved and doted upon.

Because the child is just discovering that he is a separate person from his parents, he strongly asserts this independence. The wise adult allows toddlers to explore and make choices within a safe environment. We give freedom within the security of limits and a loving, trusting relationship.

Parents must to step back and allow toddlers to do things for themselves. As they gain hand coordination, toddlers enjoy fine-motor tasks, such as puzzles and stringing beads. With carefully selected containers to practice pouring, even very young children can develop fine eye-hand control. They also enjoy the challenge of cooking and can help prepare food.

LANGUAGE DEVELOPMENT

Infants gain understanding long before they can speak. They must be exposed to language as adults talk to them and explain what is happening. When we say things like, "I'm going to change your diaper," they gradually begin to understand.

By twelve months of age, children are experimenting with their voices, imitating sounds, and saying a few words. Adults must talk and listen to the child and provide language materials such as books, objects, and pictures.

RESPECTING MISTAKES AS PART OF GROWTH

Children's development is driven by their own efforts. They look to us, believing we are wise, but our efforts to protect them from mistakes can hinder their learning. Mistakes are a natural part of learning. As parents, we must respect their efforts to develop independence. We must also understand their psychological needs. Creating a supportive home environment is crucial, but it's equally important to be patient and empathetic.

Many parents and teachers assume that children develop character through our care and upbringing. We believe we can shape a child's personality and destiny through our sound advice and efforts. Instead, children carry within themselves the key to their development. Their early attempts to express their individuality may be tentative. Our role as parents is to guide them through this process with understanding and patience, instilling in them a sense of confidence in their own abilities.

Dr. Montessori was concerned that parents would unconsciously hinder and frustrate their child's spiritual growth process, although we may operate from the best of intentions. We tend to overprotect, not realizing that our children can only learn about life through experience, just as we did.

Our role as parents is to help our children learn to live in peace and harmony with themselves, other people, and the environment. We work to create a home in which our children can learn to function as independent, thinking people. We must treat our children with tremendous respect, as complete human beings who happen to be in our care. Our children need to feel that it is okay to be themselves.

Children must feel our respect; it is not enough to say the words. If our children believe they are not living up to our expectations and that we are disappointed in the people they are becoming, they may be emotionally scarred for a lifetime. A child who feels unaccepted by their parents can only wander through life looking in from the outside, like a stranger.

PARENTS TEACH CHILDREN VALUES

One fundamental aim as parents is to inspire our children's hearts. We teach our values, ethics, and a sense of what is truly remarkable and important: love, kindness, joy, and confidence in the fundamental goodness of life.

Everything we do is intended to nurture within our children a sense of joy and appreciation of life, a sense of the poetic, and humanity's interrelationship with the universe.

We want to teach our children to understand and respect the differences among different cultures. To build a peaceful world, we must learn to see people as they are and not be afraid of what is different. Just as children can learn to hate from their parents, they can also learn to love. Children can easily realize that diversity is a call for celebration, not a cause for alarm.

We should present an honest picture of the world according to children's growing ability to understand. Naturally, though, they learn more from what we do than from what we preach. Our actions should be consistent with our values. For children to grow emotionally and morally, they must be able to trust and understand the important adults in their lives. Ultimately, they learn to

think and judge for themselves. But they begin with us as their example.

To live happily as an adult, a child needs two things: a strong sense of her identity, separate from her parents, and a sense of her full membership in her family and larger community.

Our moral obligation is to facilitate the transition from childhood to maturity and teach the skills it takes to function successfully in school, college, the workplace, and our cultural environment.

POSITIVE DISCIPLINE: ESTABLISHING A CLIMATE OF LOVE

Children are extremely sensitive to the emotional climate within the family. They love us and want us to be pleased with them. This doesn't mean that they will always behave. Every child will test the rules. In fact, most acts of testing parents are a normal part of growing up.

When children test adults, it is often their way of expressing feelings they don't understand. From our responses, they gradually learn to handle their emotions appropriately. By testing the limits, they discover that we care about specific ground rules of grace and courtesy in our relationship. In acting out, they take their first tentative steps toward independence, attempting to demonstrate that we don't control them completely.

Agree on your family ground rules and write them down. Be consistent! If you can't bring yourself to reinforce a rule again and again, it shouldn't be a ground rule at your home. A few good rules are much better than dozens of nitpicking rules that no one can remember. The Montessori home may have ground rules such as the following.

- Be kind and gentle and treat all life with respect.
- Don't whine!
- Tell the truth, and don't be afraid to admit when you make a mistake. Just do your best to learn from it.
- If you break something, clean it up.

Organize a place in the family room where your children can work or play.

Threats and punishments are not good tools to get children to behave. From our experience, children who respond to threats and punishments are anxious to please us and win back our love. On the other hand, when children are angry or asserting their independence, they often act out and don't care if they are punished.

Punishment is less effective than we assume. At both home and school, teach children to do things correctly and emphasize the positive rather than using insults and anger. It's not always easy. Above all else, try not to ask unanswerable questions, such as, "How many times do I have to tell you . . . ?" to which the appropriate response is, "I don't know, Dad! How many times do you have to tell me?"

Children are so sensitive and impressionable that we should monitor everything we say and do, for everything is engraved in their memories. Our children love us with profound affection. When they go to bed, they want us to stay with them as they sleep. When we work in the kitchen, they often want to help. We may worry that we'll spoil them if we listen to their pleas, but we shouldn't. They only want us to pay attention to them. They want to be part of the group.

Parents become frustrated in their efforts to keep peace in their homes. They concentrate on trying to get their children to do what they want instead of nurturing the family ties. Children need to be respected as independent human beings. Discipline should be taught as a series of positive lessons conducted by loving, confident parents who know their children are basically good and capable of doing the right thing. Children tend to live up to our expectations.

Love is not enough; the key is the respect we give children and insist on in return. Do not ask your children to earn your respect and trust. Assume that they deserve to be treated with respect from the beginning. Sometimes parents try to be best friends with their children, which tends to be a mistake. Children will have many friends throughout their lives but only one set of parents. If we get caught up in having our children like us, we will find it difficult to confront them when they act out of line (as they will sooner or later).

Getting angry with parents is part of growing up. It's how we create distance from our childhood.

A parent should be loved, respected, and someone to confide in, not a buddy or playmate.

Speak to the best within your child. Try to call forth the young adult who will someday walk in her shoes. Respect should extend to your child's interests and activities. Pay attention to the things that fascinate her and try to understand them.

Process over Product

We often respond to our children with, "Good job!" when they show us something. We should watch out for this, or we will raise children addicted to praise. What's wrong with praising children, you ask?

Praise is an extrinsic reward. Your child does something to get your attention and praise. But young children are motivated to create, explore, and learn for their own sake. For them, the process of doing something is more important than the product. In a conventional preschool, children bring home workbooks or art projects almost daily.

In Montessori, you may go days between seeing something come home. Children spend much of the day working with the Montessori learning materials. The process catches their attention, but no paper documents it. Young children learn through hands-on experience. They manipulate materials and gradually internalize each concept.

Occasionally, children will be excited to bring home a painting, drawing, or other work, but it is just as likely that they will give it to a friend or forget it in their cubby.

Avoid falling into the praise routine when your children bring something home or show you something they have learned. Instead, consider expressing gratitude. "Is that for me? Thank you. Did you enjoy writing this? Tell me more." In this way, you can engage your child without getting them addicted to your approval and praise. Appreciation and inquiry go a long way. "What bright colors you chose! Tell me more about your painting."

One family made this space in the living room for their young child.

ORGANIZING YOUR HOME

We must give the child an environment that he can utilize by himself: a little washstand of his own, a bureau with drawers he can open, objects of common use that he can operate, a small bed in which he can sleep at night under an attractive blanket he can fold and spread by himself.

—Dr. Maria Montessori

Bedrooms

Children's bedrooms should reflect their personalities and current interests. Even though many young children tend to create chaos on their own, they have a tremendous need and love for an orderly environment. Everything should have its place, and the environment should be organized to make it easy for the child to maintain a neat, well-organized atmosphere.

Ideally, the young child's bed is low to the floor, making it easy to get in and out independently. For babies and toddlers, consider a futon or a mattress without a bed frame instead of a crib. Some young children use a sleeping bag instead of sheets and blankets on their bed, which makes it easy for them to make their bed in the morning.

Mount a little coat and hat rack low on one wall, where your child can reach them easily. Decorate the walls with high-quality art prints of children or animals hung at the child's eye level. Hang a bulletin board at your child's eye level for artwork and school papers.

A child's bedroom

A Montessori floor bed allows very young children to move about their room as they become mobile.

Mount a wall clock at the child's level. Select one with a large, easy-to-read face.

Modify light switches with extenders to allow the young child to turn lights on and off independently.

Avoid clutter by placing toys with many pieces in appropriate containers, such as baskets, sturdy bags, or plastic tubs with lids. Use a sturdy wooden crate to hold building blocks.

Store plastic building bricks in a large, colorful, sturdy canvas bag with handles. Sew on strips of hook and loop tape to fasten the bag closed. When you travel, it is easy to pick up the bag and bring it along.

Create a model town or farm on a piece of heavy plywood. Paint it green and sprinkle model railroad "grass" on it to simulate a meadow. Placed on a low table, your child can create beautiful displays with model buildings made of wood or plastic. Add little trees and people from a model railroad set. You could set up a dollhouse this way as well.

Ensure your child's clothes chest has drawers that are the right height for them to open and look inside. Label the drawers for underwear, socks, and other items.

Collect flower vases and encourage your child to collect flowers from fields or a garden.

Provide shelf space for a small nature museum in your child's room. Here, he can display rocks, interesting seeds, and (in small cages) interesting "critters."

Music should be part of every child's life. Make space for a simple stereo system and collection of recordings.

A standing chalkboard encourages writing and drawing practice and is less messy than paint. You can buy larger chalk, perfect for young hands.

Some children enjoy this practical life exercise at home, gathering water in a pitcher, pouring it into a basin, and using it to wash their hands, just as they do in their Montessori classroom.

Bathrooms

The bathroom must be prepared for your children. They should be able to turn on the water and reach their toothbrush and toothpaste without help. There should be a special place for their towel and wash-cloth. Most parents provide bathroom stools, but small, wobbly stools may not be secure or comfortable enough for bathroom tasks. You might consider building a wooden platform 6 to 8 inches (15 to 20 cm) high that fits around the toilet and sink.

Arts and Crafts

Set up an art area with an easel and a table for drawing, craftwork, and clay. Cover the table with a washable tablecloth.

Children's art supplies can be neatly stored in plastic containers. Depending on your child's age, art supplies might include washable markers, crayons, paste, paper, fabric scraps, and recycled household materials for making collages.

Bathroom adaptations can encourage young children's independence.

A child painting at a home easel

Some families allow children, wearing safety goggles, to practice using a hammer and nail on an old log.

This family constructed a small kitchen work area for their child to help prepare food.

Kitchens

Make room in your kitchen for a child-sized work table or a stepstool. Set aside the bottom shelf in your refrigerator for your children. Here, you can store small drink pitchers, fruit, and ingredients for making sandwiches and snacks.

Use nonbreakable containers to hold peanut butter, jam, lunch meats, and spreads. Two-year-olds can open the refrigerator to get their prepared snack or cold drink. Slightly older children can pour their own juice and make their own lunch. Use a bottom drawer to hold forks, knives, and spoons. Mount a low plate, cup, and napkin shelf on a wall.

Using small dishes, glasses, and silverware, young children prepare their own snacks.

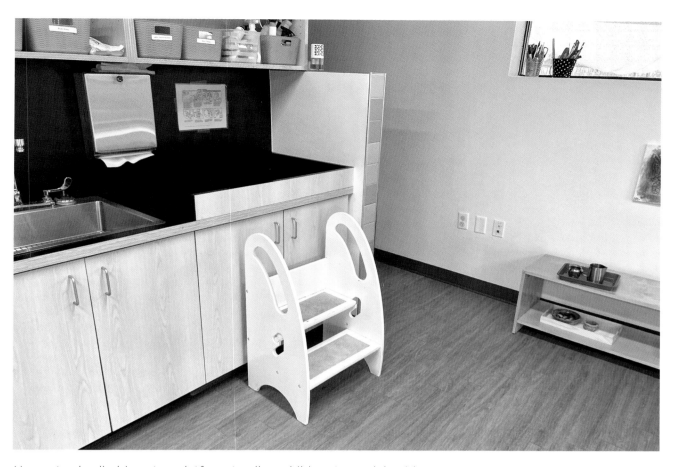

Use a sturdy climbing step platform to allow children to work beside you.

Young children enjoy eating snacks or working at child-sized tables.

Young children may enjoy helping to clean windows.

Helping around the House

If activities are presented correctly, children as young as two delight in caring for their environment: dusting, mopping, scrubbing, cleaning, and polishing. They should be able to do so as easily at home as at school. It is reasonable to ask older children to straighten up their rooms and help with simple household chores.

- Give your child their own little broom or small vacuum.
- Hang a feather duster on a hook.
- Provide a hamper for dirty clothes. Ask your child to carry them to the laundry room regularly.
- The bathroom should have a small bucket, scrub brush, and sponge.
- Folding towels and napkins is a good activity for young children.

PREPARING FOR HOLIDAYS AND CELEBRATIONS

Children are an integral part of the family and should play a meaningful role in planning and preparing for holidays and family celebrations. According to their age, children can clean their rooms, chop vegetables, help with cooking and baking, set the table, carry food to the table, set out holiday decorations, receive guests at the door, sit nicely at the table, and act as hosts to young friends and relatives visiting their home. We are all pleased when friends and relatives compliment us on our children's intelligence, charm, and courtesy.

TELEVISION AND DIGITAL DEVICES

Children's values and knowledge about the world have traditionally been shaped by four cultural influences: home, school, church, and peer groups. Today, television and digital media represent a compelling fifth influence over which most of us have scant knowledge and exercise little control. This is unfortunate, especially considering that it has become the babysitter of choice in many families.

There are several problems with uncontrolled screen time and children. The violence portrayed on television is tremendously concerning. In one year, a child can see thousands of murders, fights, car crashes, and explosions. They are exposed to sexualized content at an early age. Cyberbullying is also a problem. The values and problem-solving approaches that video game developers and media producers consider appropriate differ from our own. An even more significant concern is the hypnotic character of spending too much time sitting before a screen.

Many parents observe that their young children can sit and watch for hours. Of course they watch for extended periods; they are in a trance. Viewing videos or TV is, at best, a passive experience. It requires no thought, imagination, or effort. Quality children's programming can be terrific, but most of what's available is anything but. TV is best doled out in carefully planned and measured doses.

Establish family ground rules that make sense to you. Determine the shows your children can watch, and limit the number of hours a day your child can spend doing so. Give your children as much choice as possible: "You can choose from the following shows; however, you can only watch three of them in any one day. What do you want today's choices to be?"

Some families allow children to watch only public television on their own. Parents decide case by case whether commercial television shows are appropriate. Sometimes, a show may have real value, but it may have confusing or disturbing content. The whole family should watch and discuss the show together.

As much as possible, support your child's desire for activity. Don't try to wait on or entertain her. Encourage her to be independent. Be careful about what you do or say in front of children. As the well-known poem says, "Children learn what they live." They are much more sensitive to our influence than we realize. We communicate volumes about how we feel about our children by the kind of home we make for them. By including children in our family life and showing concern for their feelings and respect for their interests, we tell them how much they mean to us.

Sometimes young people become oblivious to those around them even at the dinner table.

Building and decorating a bird feeder

CHAPTER 16

Parents Working in Partnership with Schools

All schools work best when parents are engaged and supportive. This is especially true for Montessori schools. This will only work if you are informed, supportive, and working in partnership with your child's teachers and the school as a whole. If you feel that you can't or do not want to get involved or find that Montessori makes you nervous, then you may have made a mistake. Every child deserves to be in a school that their parents have chosen consciously, with confidence and wholehearted support.

To become an informed partner with your child's new Montessori school, begin by familiarizing yourself with the core principles of Montessori education. See the Resources section of this book for recommendations.

Additionally, many Montessori schools offer resources such as newsletters, blogs, and recommended reading lists. These materials can deepen your understanding and keep you informed about the school's educational practices and events.

ENGAGE WITH THE SCHOOL COMMUNITY

Building a relationship with the school community is vital for a successful partnership. Here are some ways to get involved.

Attend events. Participate in workshops, seminars, and informational sessions hosted by the school. These are designed to help parents understand the Montessori method and its application in the classroom.

Join parent groups. These associations can provide a support network and opportunities to learn from experienced parents.

Volunteer. Whether you help with classroom activities, assist at school events, or participate in committees, your involvement will demonstrate your commitment to your child's education.

Many schools invite parents to volunteer in the classroom.

FOSTER OPEN COMMUNICATION

Effective communication with your child's teachers and school staff is crucial for addressing concerns and supporting your child's development. Here are some tips for fostering open communication.

Introduce yourself. Get to know your child's teachers and school staff. Building a positive rapport early on will make future conversations more comfortable and productive.

Schedule regular check-ins. Meetings with teachers can provide valuable insights into your child's progress and any areas of concern. These are opportunities to discuss observations, ask questions, and collaborate on strategies to support your child's development.

BECOME AN INFORMED PARENT PARTNER

To become an informed parent partner, it's important to continuously educate yourself, stay engaged with the school community, and maintain open lines of communication. Here are some additional steps you can take.

Observe your child. Pay close attention to your child's behavior and progress at school and home. Journaling about your observations can be helpful when discussing concerns with teachers.

Seek clarification. If you find any aspects of the Montessori method confusing, don't hesitate to ask teachers to explain. Most educators are happy to discuss their approach.

Stay open-minded. Montessori education can be quite different from traditional methods. Trust the process and allow time to see results. Be receptive to new ideas and approaches, and remember that your child's educational journey is unique.

ADDRESS CONCERNS POSITIVELY

When concerns arise, addressing them positively and constructively is essential for maintaining a solid partnership with the school. Here are some strategies:

Approach conversations with empathy and understanding. Teachers and school staff are working in your child's best interest. Be willing to listen to their observations and ideas.

Be specific and objective. Clearly articulate your concerns with specific examples and observations. Avoid making generalizations or letting emotions drive the conversation.

Collaborate on solutions. Work with teachers to identify potential solutions. Be open to their suggestions and share your ideas. The goal is to develop a plan that supports your child's needs while aligning with the Montessori philosophy.

Follow-up. After implementing any agreed-upon solutions, follow up with teachers to assess progress and make any necessary adjustments. Regular communication will help ensure that your strategies are effective and that any further concerns can be promptly addressed.

Partnering with your child's Montessori school involves active participation, continuous learning, and open communication. By preparing yourself with knowledge, engaging with the school community, and maintaining a collaborative approach, you can effectively support your child's educational journey. Remember, the goal is to work together with the school to create a positive and enriching experience for your child.

CHAPTER 17

Montessori for Learners with Exceptionalities

By Ann Epstein, professor of Montessori education at the University of Wisconsin

Note: The photos used to illustrate this chapter represent common scenes of Montessori teachers and students. They were not chosen because they have any learning exceptionalities. Children are children, and most students who have a special need do not look different from their peers. Montessori teachers strive to make every child feel honored, accepted, and successful.

While Montessori schools cannot offer one-on-one instruction, teachers know their students exceptionally well and can call them aside for individual or small-group support.

All parents seek learning environments that match their children's strengths and needs. One of the most crucial responsibilities of parenthood is to ensure that children are able to learn and grow in an environment that is both challenging and nurturing. Parents watch over their children's academic and social progress every day. Moreover, they have the reward of watching their children grow and succeed.

However, parents of children who learn differently (or perhaps look, move, or talk differently) have an extra set of challenges. The neighborhood public schools may or may not provide an atmosphere that matches their child's learning style. They need a school that preserves the child's interest in learning, passion, happiness, and self-confidence in spite of any perceived challenges.

Society has begun to recognize the importance of providing accommodations and inclusion for children who are exceptional in their physical, social, or cognitive development learning style or who find it difficult to interact with others. The

term *neurodivergent* describes the idea that human brains and neurological development are not uniform and follow a wide range of paths. Education and society as a whole must recognize these differences and then do what we can to address these needs.

Quite a few types of differences can affect learning. Here are some of the most common.

- Learning disabilities, which can make reading, writing, and math difficult
- Attention deficit disorder (ADD) and attention deficit hyperactivity disorder (ADHD)
- Speech or language disabilities
- Developmental delays
- Emotional and behavioral disabilities and mental illness
- Health impairments
- Deafness or hearing loss
- Orthopedic impairments
- Blindness or low vision
- Autism spectrum disorder (ASD)
- Traumatic brain injuries

Special educators urge parents and education professionals to consider each child a unique individual, which is also a central tenet of the Montessori philosophy. Each child with a disability is unique, with their own specific strengths and areas of weakness.

Many parents come to Montessori schools after an educational experience that has not nurtured their child's individual needs, leaving the child and family hurt, apprehensive, and possibly even traumatized.

What attracts these parents to Montessori? They may have heard about Montessori's principles of choice and independence. Many children thrive in this kind of learning environment. Self-determination is particularly important for children who have disabilities. One child may be interested in experimenting with objects that either sink or float, while another may decide to wash, peel, slice, and serve celery. A child may have learned that the number twelve is comprised of one, ten, and two units and wants to learn more.

With appropriate guidance from teachers, hundreds of choices are available. Students form the essential lifelong characteristics of being independent thinkers and accepting responsibility for their own choices.

These two learning characteristics are key protectors against parents' natural tendency to be overprotective of their exceptional children. The prepared learning environment is carefully designed to provide the opportunity to choose activities that attract children's curiosity.

A Montessori education allows children with different learning styles to build confidence when they might otherwise feel put down. Confidence encourages children to advocate for themselves, make choices, take on challenges, and navigate a world filled with opportunities for action.

The fit between the Montessori philosophy and children with disabilities is rooted in two essential responsibilities. The teacher must observe and understand each child's style of learning. Throughout the day, Montessori teachers watch how children respond to lessons and pursue independent activities. They note which activities bring delight and those that lead to frustration.

As children progress, expectations and goals change to meet their developmental needs. Montessori guides observe where children are developmentally, taking into consideration the child's challenges and nuances.

They watch how children interact with one another and with adults. Are some children demonstrating emerging signs of leadership skills? Do others struggle to express their thoughts and feelings? Are there patterns to children's challenging behaviors? For instance, do they happen at a particular time of day, with some children but not with others, or during transitions?

Montessori teachers also carefully prepare the learning environment. Each day, children choose from dozens of activities designed for independent, successful learning. Thus, children will meet with success rather than frustration.

The principle of learning task analysis, or breaking each skill into sequential parts, helps children develop skills and understanding step by step. For example, learning to tie shoes can be daunting for children with fine motor delays. The teacher designs bead stringing and lacing activities to build eye-hand coordination. Gluing, working with clay, and painting also build fine motor skills.

The experience of working with interesting, frustration-free, self-chosen activities gradually builds skills and self-confidence. Eventually, children become comfortable with the first step in making a shoestring loop. With practice, bit by bit, they learn to make a second loop, wrap it around the first, tuck it through a special space, pull it through, and create that long-sought bow!

DOES THE MONTESSORI APPROACH FIT SPECIAL EDUCATION BEST PRACTICES?

Fundamental principles of early intervention and special education are embedded in many Montessori environments. Teachers and parents must understand the child's present levels of performance to address needs and build strengths of a learner with a disability.

Although Montessori teachers are not usually trained or certified to perform standardized tests of cognition, physical, or social-emotional development, they bring detailed information from their ongoing observations to planning meetings. Combining their classroom observations with parents' observations and evaluation and assessment results creates a rich understanding of the child's performance levels.

Special educators develop measurable short-term objectives to guide daily classroom learning. Montessori teachers break skills and concepts into

sequential steps. Sequenced activities fit well into an exceptional learner's short-term objectives.

The special educator builds these activities into a schedule of day-to-day lessons, noting when Sally is successful and when she experiences difficulty. Her errors will be analyzed to identify where her understanding breaks down. When Sally is able to complete nine of ten problems successfully, the objective will be marked complete.

HOW TO ASSESS WHETHER THIS MONTESSORI SCHOOL IS A GOOD FIT FOR YOUR CHILD

Initially, parents and teachers decide whether a Montessori environment is the best setting for the child. To assess the potential for a successful placement, they examine characteristics of both the school and the child.

Montessori schools can offer a positive experience for children with disabilities. However, schools vary in how they apply Montessori principles. Perhaps more importantly, administrative and faculty capacity to include children with disabilities also varies. Indeed, each child's disability presents unique challenges to their family and school setting.

The following questions may help determine whether a particular Montessori school would provide a positive experience for a child with disabilities.

Questions for the Family

- Are the teacher and the administration willing to make changes to accommodate my child's unique needs? Would they shorten lessons, modify homework, provide behavioral support, or assure wheelchair accessibility?
- Do the teacher and the administration seem comfortable explaining my child's special needs to their classmates so my child can make friends?
- Will the school work collaboratively with my child's therapists, such as family counselors or speech, occupational, or physical therapists?
- Do I feel welcomed and included when my child and I are in the school?
- Can I picture my child feeling welcomed and included in the classroom?

A computer or tablet can be a useful assistive device for some students, such as those who struggle to write legibly or who use voice dictation to compose written material.

One simple accommodation is to encourage a student who feels distracted to work in an alcove or wear sound-canceling headphones.

Questions for the School

- Do we (teachers, administration, and, if appropriate, support or specialist teachers) fully understand the child's exceptionality?
- Has the family shared relevant reports and test results?
- Are we willing to make accommodations within the classroom, such as modifying lessons, assisting with choosing work, providing behavioral support, or ensuring wheelchair accessibility?
- Can we modify the environment throughout the school, such as in the cafeteria, playground, hallways, or gym, to provide necessary support for the child?
- Do we understand how to help the child progress cognitively and socially and emotionally? If not, are we willing to learn how to provide the necessary assistance?

Answers to these questions are often "Maybe," "I think so," or "We will do our best." Absolute yeses are not necessary for the child to be successful. Honest discussions and solid planning, however, are essential. Families and schools need to understand one another's abilities and limitations.

If the above questions have been discussed and admission is agreed upon, parents and educators can look forward to a potentially transforming experience. Teachers who questioned their ability to meet the needs of children with disabilities but agreed to welcome them anyway often report the experience as among their most rewarding. They report the accomplishment of implementing new teaching strategies and the joy of seeing the child progress.

One gratifying aspect for families is their children's relationship with peers. Other children in the classroom tend to demonstrate leadership, kindness, heartfelt interest, and sometimes ingenuity as they develop an understanding of their classmates' disabilities.

Along with success, parents and educators often encounter challenges and frustrations. It is essential to keep communications open while consistently monitoring the outcome of varied teaching strategies. The following questions may assist the parent-educator team in maintaining progress.

Self-confidence is a gift.

Questions for the Family

- Am I staying informed of my child's progress with regular communications between school and home? Teachers and families can choose from a wide variety of options, including email, phone calls, face-to-face meetings, and daily journals. They must find tools and methods that work well for their partnership.
- Do we understand and support the current objectives and strategies used to attain them?
- Is my child participating successfully in both classroom and auxiliary activities, such as art or physical education?
- Are my child's teacher and therapists sharing regular updates?
- Do I have a clear understanding of what teaching methods are working well for my child?
- If my child is not making progress, do I understand what changes are being proposed? Do I agree with these changes? Is there a clear plan for implementing these changes and then assessing their success?

Questions for the School

- Do we have a clear understanding of the child's current learning and behavioral objectives?
- Do we share regular updates with the family?
- Are we maintaining consistent communications with the child's therapists? Are teaching strategies consistent across school, therapy, and home environments?
- Is the child making steady progress?
- If the child is not making steady progress, are we working collaboratively with parents to identify alternative teaching strategies? Once these strategies are implemented, are we communicating regularly with the family to assess progress?
- If alternatives are not successful, are we providing the family with comprehensive assistance in transitioning to a new school setting?

All children eventually reach the point of transition from their current learning setting. For most, this transition occurs because the child has made steady progress and outgrown the current program. For some, the setting is no longer a good fit for their particular strengths and needs. In both situations, the learner's success depends on careful planning by educators and families. The following questions can help transition students into new situations.

Questions for the Family

- Do I fully understand my child's present levels of performance across all learning areas (cognitive, social-emotional, language, motor)?
- If I am unsure of my child's present levels of performance, what resources can I access to arrange for quality assessments?
- Do I understand and agree with current learning objectives and long-range goals for my child? If not, have I communicated my concerns and begun the process of reassessing objectives and goals with my child's teacher and therapists?
- Do I know about other learning environments in my community that could provide a better setting for my child?
- Have I met with teachers and administrators at other potential schools?
- Has a meeting been arranged between my child's present teacher and their new teacher to discuss current performance levels?
- Is my child (when appropriate) involved with the transition?
- Have we planned for my child to visit their new school several times while still enrolled in our current school?
- Have we planned for my child to say goodbye to classmates?
- Have all my child's records been transferred to our new school?
- Have I shared my feelings (whether positive or negative) and bid farewell with a sense of completion and peace?

Questions for the School

- Are the child's records current, including present performance levels across all learning domains, clearly stated objectives, and clearly documented teaching strategies?
- Have we shared information with the family about potential schools in our community?

- Have we helped the family arrange a meeting with the potential school's administrator and teacher to share information about the child's learning style and successful strategies?
- Have we worked with the family to arrange visits to the child's new school?
- Have we planned when and how the child will say goodbye to classmates?
- Have we met with the family to share final farewells, providing an atmosphere where all share both positive and negative feelings?
- If necessary, have we documented any changes to school policy or procedures based on our experiences with the family?

Schools should keep in mind several questions throughout the child's time with the Montessori community.
- Are all meetings, changes, assessments, and conversations documented?
- Does the family consistently have access to resources such as websites, high-quality apps, current literature, other parent contacts, community resources, and professional workshops?
- Are we staying informed of best practices for children with disabilities?

LEARNING IN THE MONTESSORI ENVIRONMENT

The experiences of families of children with special needs vary significantly from school to school and even from environment to environment within the same school. Many Montessori teachers welcome the opportunity to adapt their environments to meet children's needs. Others are uncomfortable with adaptations, remarking that they are not trained or that the Montessori classroom is not suited to respond to special learning needs. Parents must select a Montessori community that embraces children with varying strengths and areas of need.

Assuming that the family has selected a school with an inclusive philosophy, what is the day-to-day experience of a child with a disability in a Montessori environment? The following vignettes provide brief glimpses into Montessori environments.

It is a gift to be allowed to grow at your own pace and have individual time with your teacher when you need help.

Justin

Six-year-old Justin is beginning the lower elementary program. In a traditional school, he would be in first grade. He has twenty-two classmates, ranging in age from six to nine and distributed across first, second, and third grade. Because children work at their own pace, there is considerable variation as to who is in what group for math, language, science, and social studies lessons.

Justin's early childhood teachers expressed concern that he was not able to build three- and four-letter phonetic words or recognize sight words at the end of his kindergarten year. They suggested a comprehensive academic assessment. Results suggest that Justin may have a reading disability, although his math skills are higher than those of other children his age.

In his Montessori program, Justin avoids working with the language materials. He complains about composing words with the moveable alphabet and consistently needs more time to read word and phrase cards. His teachers know he loves soccer and enjoys preparing food. They create a series of matching words and pictures around these two interests, help him write a survey about soccer for his classmates, and guide him in creating a collage depicting the steps of making a pizza. They also encourage his parents to continue periodic testing and to consider tutoring services. They all agree that now is the time to build Justin's self-confidence by building his math strengths rather than over-emphasizing catch-up work in language.

Sarah

Four-year-old Sarah smiles often, loves modeling clay, enjoys books and puzzles, and likes to run on the playground. She does not speak, and she is learning sign language with her parents. Sarah has Down syndrome and works with both occupational and speech therapists. Her Montessori teachers have learned simple signs for feelings, objects, and activities in the classroom. They ask Sarah if she is happy or sad today, remind her to hang up her coat, and teach her about colors, numbers, mammals, and sink versus float using gestures, a few signs, and lots of facial expressions.

Sarah's classmates enjoy teaching her how to pour, scoop, and wash sea shells. They learn to be patient when she spills rice or drips water, reminding her to clean up spills. Frustrations occur when Sarah cannot clearly communicate what she wants or needs, despite the community's willingness to use sign language. Her teachers, parents, and therapists continually review all the available learning options, from adapting lessons in the Montessori school to visiting classrooms in the public school system. Even though most days go fairly well, they realize a time may come when Sarah's needs will be better met in another educational setting.

Sam

Ten-year-old Sam likes to explore chemical reactions. He has cerebral palsy and uses a motorized wheelchair to navigate the various curriculum areas in his classroom. He works hard to communicate clearly, and his classmates can usually understand his speech. He uses a keyboard attached to his wheelchair tray to slowly type words and phrases when people cannot understand his speech. Sam is also gifted and attends a science enrichment class at the university in his town. His parents have both modified their career plans to give themselves more time to transport Sam to his therapies and classes.

Although Sam excels academically, he struggles to make friends. He had playmates when he was a preschooler, but as he grew older, his peers began to play without him. Although they were polite, they did not know how to adapt activities so he could participate. As the years went by, they felt guilty that Sam was usually on the edge of the playground and not invited to birthdays and overnights. Sam often feels left out and lonely; his teachers and parents worry that he may become depressed.

His physical therapist suggests a program called Circle of Friends, which would provide a structure to improve Sam's social life. They hope the program will benefit both Sam and his classmates. They know that Sam has a wacky sense of humor. They want him to feel happier and be part of the class community, but they need help learning how to be his friend.

Shana

Shana's mother felt lucky to find a Montessori school that agreed to accept her daughter. Reports from Shana's previous school say that although she was usually attentive and respectful, her behavior required constant management. Medication helps her manage her hyperactivity. Since turning six, Shana has started to recognize upsetting situations and ask for help instead of yelling or pushing. Her Montessori teachers help her make charts and record her own behaviors.

She stays focused during morning circle time and the morning work period, except when she pushed three-year-old Jake to get to the snack table. She feels proud that she asked permission to leave the group lesson on China after trying her best to listen without tickling and wrestling with Lana, who was sitting next to her. She knew it would disturb Lana and the other children and that she could have a lesson from a classmate later.

Shana's teachers work with a behavior specialist to learn self-management strategies. Already keen observers, they often catch Shana "being good," so they know she is aware of appropriate behaviors. They watch for early signs of inattentive or disrespectful behaviors and teach Shana how to spot these red flags herself. Not all days go well, particularly when the class routine changes for a visitor or special celebration. Shana's teachers have told her mom that they are concerned about spending so much more time with Shana than with the other children.

All are hopeful that Shana will learn to manage her own behavior. They know that a change might be needed if Shana continues to require more assistance than her teachers can offer. But they are all impressed by how quickly Shana has learned to say, "I need to go listen to an audio-book," instead of disrupting a group lesson. They want Shana to succeed.

Montessori is not the answer for all children who have disabilities. Justin, Sarah, Sam, and Shana have wonderful days and not-so-wonderful days in their classrooms. Their parents and teachers work hard to understand their strengths and needs and adapt the curriculum to create the best fit possible. They recognize the potential Montessori has for children with disabilities and are committed to creating positive experiences for each child. And they are aware of the constant need to communicate honestly: what is going well, what is not going well, what can we do differently, and is this the best environment for this child at this time?

Several studies offer examples of how the Montessori approach to learning assists children with disabilities as well as those who have learning and behavioral challenges but are not identified as disabled. In 2021, Tiyraki found that Montessori preschool children in Turkey were found to score higher in self-regulation and attention/impulse control. McDonell (2017) studied special education schools in Hyderabad, India, concluding that the noncompetitive nature of Montessori education is effective for many learners with disabilities. Children, both with and without disabilities, help and encourage one another while working at their own pace. Developing social skills is particularly challenging for children on the autism spectrum. Epstein et al. (2020) described how members of Montessori classroom communities often learn to assist children who are autistic as they engage in class-wide cooking projects and play together during outside time.

Long et al. (2021) surveyed eighty U.S. Montessori school heads, who revealed that children with disabilities comprise 8.5 percent of primary classrooms and 3.5 percent of infant/toddler learning environments. Language and speech are the most frequently occurring disabilities. Autism and ADHD were next.

PART SIX

Pulling It All Together

CHAPTER 18

Reflections on Montessori

Following are stories and thoughts from parents, former students, and educators, reflecting on their experience with Montessori education. Some are recent, and others are from thirty years ago.

"Montessori is warm and fuzzy. Children enjoy it, but the real world isn't warm and fuzzy. They have to grow up sometime."

"I'm worried that Montessori shelters my child from life."

"Your children are still in Montessori? You should be thinking about their future. You do want them to go to college, don't you?"

Montessori parents often hear comments like these from well-meaning relatives, coworkers, or neighbors. When it comes to Montessori, everyone has an opinion.

As their children grow, many Montessori parents find themselves defending their choice to keep their children in Montessori. Relatives' opinions are often the most difficult to discount because these people are legitimately concerned about their grandchildren or nieces and nephews.

The pressure can be enormous. Many times, we were tempted to leave Montessori and put our children in the capable hands of a more traditional school. After all, we turned out all right—or did we?

Personally, I question how we as a society have come to define success. Is a child growing up to be a doctor or a lawyer any more successful than a carpenter, musician, teacher, or homemaker? Do many well-intentioned parents unconsciously push their children into high-status careers that we as a society have come to accept as the true measure of success?

Does it matter to us that our children grow up to be happy with their choice in career, have a sense of fulfillment every day they go to work, approach each day with enthusiasm and eagerness, accept the challenges that life has to offer, and adapt to new ideas and technology? If we as parents can answer yes to these questions, then our children are well placed in a Montessori environment for as long as we can keep them there.

When we designed the first cover of our Montessori family magazine, *Tomorrow's Child*, thirty years ago, we tried to find a provocative way to portray the question: Does Montessori prepare children for the real world?

The cover we chose has a great deal of personal significance to me. First, the boy in the picture is my son, Robin, at age twelve. I can assure you he did not dress like that in real life. Second, it was the first time I ever succeeded in getting him into a tie and jacket long enough to have a picture taken.

But the third reason is most important. As a young adult, I chose a career in law for all the wrong reasons. I believed that becoming a lawyer

Tomorrow's Child *magazine, January 1993*

would give me prestige and wealth. What it actually gave me was an ulcer and the nagging feeling that I should be doing something else with my life. Please don't get me wrong. I don't dislike lawyers. There is nothing wrong with the law, medicine, teaching, carpentry, or anything else as long as it is what is right for the individual.

But back to whether or not Montessori prepares children for the real world. If the answer is to be judged by whether or not great percentages of Montessori students will pursue professional careers, then the answer is maybe. For example, Steph Curry, the NBA MVP who plays with the Golden State Warriors, was a Montessori child.

Today, my son has a doctorate and is a senior consultant with the Montessori Foundation. He has been very successful in business, educational leadership, and Montessori teacher training.

At fifteen, Robin's sister told us she wanted to work for the FBI, carry a gun, and project power. Today, she has a doctorate in forensic psychology and works in the criminal justice system.

If the answer to the question is whether Montessori prepares children for life, though, the answer is unequivocal: Yes!

As a parent, I had very high expectations for my children from Montessori. I expected them to be well-prepared academically so they could follow whatever dreams they had, but I also hoped they would continue making responsible choices. I care about academics, but I knew my children would get that from any good school, Montessori or otherwise. For me, the value of Montessori went beyond academics.

I often wish I could have had a Montessori experience as a child. Things might have turned out differently. For one thing, I could have saved all that money on law school, but I believe all learning experiences have value. A bit of Montessori did rub off on me, after all. At age 35, I quit the practice of law and went on to do something much more fulfilling, something I may have done earlier if I had not tried so hard to jam my round-pegged personality into a square professional hole.

When I announced that I wasn't going to practice law anymore, the initial overwhelming response was, "What do you mean you're not going to practice law anymore? How do you think you're going to survive in the real world without a profession?" Sound familiar?

More than anything, I hope we as parents will have the courage to recognize and continue supporting the human values and life lessons our children are learning daily in their Montessori classrooms. Our world could use many more Montessori lawyers, politicians, and doctors who understand there's more to life than being book smart.

The Montessori classroom is very true to life. Children pursue their interests in the context of choice. Montessori children see their own growth and respond to their own needs.

—Joyce St. Giermaine, executive director of the Montessori Foundation, editor of *Tomorrow's Child* magazine, an attorney, and the mother of two former Montessori students

Above all, though, our objective as parents and educators is not to teach children to survive in the real world. We should help them learn to celebrate life and how to make the world a better place.

They learn to make individual choices that connect with their capabilities. The Montessori classroom allows for diverse individual expressions, personalities, and cultural origins. We must broaden the images of success to include roles such as carpenter, welder, automotive mechanic, beautician, and poet.

Some say that Montessori classrooms are devoid of competition and, therefore, not part of the real world. Still, competition, like cooperation, is natural to life and thus emerges naturally in the Montessori classroom. Children freely compare and contrast their work. Montessorians are careful not to exploit the natural competition but to note how children build or lose self-esteem in relation to how they perceive themselves or others.

I would hardly consider the Montessori classroom a shelter from the real world. In this microsociety, children learn a great deal about human nature and individual personality.

They learn tolerance and respect as modeled by the Montessori-trained teacher. They learn about fairness, different approaches to different needs, and individuality in relation to group cooperation.

Success is in the eyes of the beholder; it is primarily formed privately, individually, and compassionately by the child and the family. Even the Montessori classroom cannot substitute for a parent's faith in their child or the child's faith in following their own star.

—David Kahn, former executive director of the North American Montessori Teachers' Association

These students work together to prepare dinner for sixty guests.

My daughter, Anna, started Montessori at two, discovering a world of respect. Today, Anna is at Tufts University. In college, she's matching what the preschool experience in Montessori gave her. Anna speaks four languages, three of which she started as a Montessori child. Montessori allowed my child to discover that she was a very important person who could be aware of the world and become a member of the bigger human community.

—Celma Perry, former director of the MECA-Seton teacher training program, written thirty years ago. Anna is currently the director of the MECA-Seton program.

Both of my children who had Montessori education have a quality of daring and competence in their ability that has enabled them to approach new problems and challenges with appropriate confidence, great enthusiasm, and focus. This is one of the dispositional outcomes of Montessori, which has never been measured but is palpable in most parents' experiences.

—Nancy Rambusch, PhD, founder of the American Montessori Society and cofounder of the Montessori Foundation

We cannot prepare children specifically for a world that is yet to be. We live in a world of change. The only constant in our life is change. We cannot know what the world will be like when they become adults.

When teachers focus exclusively on the skills they will give children, they lose sight of the picture Montessori offered us. The whole concept of the Montessori classroom is a place where children can create themselves to their fullest potential. They are not just learning to write and read. They are developing themselves as individuals.

Two children came to me in first grade at a Mexico City school from Chihuahua, where Montessori had begun in Mexico in the 1960s. They had both been in Montessori since they were three. They went on to a middle school with 1,000 students, run by a private organization, which they started in September. In November, the children in that middle school elected their officers, electing one of these children president and the other treasurer.

Now, what a coincidence that two kids out of 1,000 who had been there all of two months were chosen by their peers to be their leaders. Montessori is not designed to make you the best mathematician or anything in that sense. It is designed to help each person become the most complete human being she can be, and all those other things come along without being the focus of our primary effort.

Montessori students often become intently focused on their work.

—Feland Meadows, PhD, former president of the Pan-American Montessori Society

From my experiences with students who leave the programs and the feedback that I get from high schools and parents, students are academically prepared. But more than that, they are fearless in taking calculated risks to try out for the play. They become student leaders directed toward activities like beginning a service project.

When given a project, these students know how to choose a topic and work it through completion while the other kids are still sitting around trying to figure out how to begin. They are self-starters and have the skills to break down and complete a task without total direction from teachers. Many of our students are becoming engineers. They win lots of math and science awards. They are going into the sciences. During significant periods in the Montessori classroom, they learned to feel good about math and sciences.

They are also the outspoken ones. They are the ones that come up with the petitions or will take a stand on moral issues.

—Elisabeth Coe, PhD, past president of the American Montessori Society and director of the Houston Montessori Center

The answer to the question of whether or not Montessori prepares children for the real world depends on what we see as the real world. If the real world is that people interact well and that we treat one another as people, not as statistics, then Montessori prepares them for the real world.

Suppose the real world is where we want people to think for themselves, figure out solutions for themselves, work in groups, and interact with other people peacefully. In that case, Montessori prepares them for it.

So we need to ask ourselves, "What type of real world do we want for the future?" and then prepare them for it. If it's global peace that we're looking for, then Montessori prepares children for it.

—Joseph Purvis, former principal of the Hall School, Minneapolis

My experience with Montessori matched how I learn best. I recently applied to a doctoral program, and one of the things that they wanted us to talk about was to situate our experience and how we got to this point. The real pivotal experiences for me were my Montessori experiences and some college experiences because Montessori allows you to become an autonomous learner for the rest of your life. You carry it on the job and bring it into any other school setting. It permits you to select what you will do, begin it, complete it, and get closure in a way you are not allowed to do in many settings. It's a very adult skill to develop.

—Alexandra Rambusch, doctoral candidate and former Montessori student, written 30 years ago

I started in Montessori at age two. I'm a product of the entire system. I did well, but still, many people wondered if I had been prepared for college and whether I could make it in a "real" school? The skepticism was so disconcerting that I never bothered to step back and see what fifteen years of trust, respect, teaching, and learning had done for me. When I went off to Northwestern University, I left my support system and community behind and entered a world that was much colder and uncaring.

At first, I deeply missed that sense of belonging. I didn't realize that Barrie had not only given me a second family but had also taught me how to build new friendships, support systems, and community wherever I go. I now use my years of experience in community building to cultivate secure relationships. Barrie did more for me than just prepare me academically for college. It prepared me for anything to which I chose to apply myself.

—Frances Merenda, sustainability engineer, graduate of the Barrie School

I went to Montessori school from eighteen months until first grade. I took a break for a couple of years and came running back as fast as possible to finish third grade through high school. I graduated in 2018 with only three other seniors and then studied electrical engineering at Georgia Tech.

I distinctly remember that we did a school project about barrier islands. We went to the beach in Florida to measure the slope of the shore and the kind of sand and rock material there. I was interested in making salt. So I brought two big 5-gallon (20 L) water jugs with me to the beach and filled them with ocean water.

My teachers let me boil ocean water in the cafeteria kitchen over the next week to concentrate the water to make flaky salt. I still use that jar of salt. I was allowed to explore my interests, and that curiosity led me to learn something you wouldn't learn in a traditional school.

I was allowed to design the school's IT infrastructure, networking, and Wi-Fi access points. I learned how to assign IP addresses to computers and other valuable skills you don't usually learn in high school.

I earned the International Baccalaureate diploma and got college credit for most of the courses I took in high school. I earned, overall, a 3.88 GPA in undergraduate electrical engineering at Georgia Tech, finishing in three and a half years. Only about 10 percent of students graduate in four years. Following our curiosity is separate from more traditional academics. It prepares you for the real world, things that aren't solving math equations, such as, how do you fix your car when it breaks down?

While our high school was small, I worked with students who were younger, older, and my age. I also got to know my teachers as people. It was a culture shock transitioning from a small Montessori high school to a large university, but I had the requisite social skills to get along with people.

Engineers take something theoretical, such as numbers and equations, and build a tangible system that represents that information. Montessori has materials that take these abstract concepts and put them into tangible formats.

It teaches that concept at a very early age, like doing long division with tiles. I remember this cube with smaller cubes and rectangles, which essentially illustrates the quadratic equation. If you can make that connection and understand its concept, you have an edge in STEM fields. Taking an abstract idea and creating something physical out of it is much more valuable and highly sought-after than churning out equations for a test.

I always enjoy telling people that I came from Montessori, with a graduating class of four people, and, yes, I'm very successful in a technical field. There are no limitations. Montessori doesn't limit you to one side of the spectrum in terms of STEM versus the arts; it does an outstanding job of teaching those skills that are required to solve problems and look for different ways to come up with a solution.

—Ben Bogard, electrical engineer at SpaceX, graduate of NewGate Montessori High School

I have always loved animals, nature, playing outside, and stuff like that. I always read books about that, like Magic Treehouse books about the jungle. And then, as I grew up, I realized I really liked science. I didn't love math as much. Environmental science is a connection between loving nature, the environment, and science.

Did any experiences from my Montessori classes encourage my study of environmental science? I remember those long timelines with drawings of early humans and all the dinosaurs, prehistoric eras, geological eras, and things like that, which interested me. When I was in Montessori kindergarten, I walked across the parking lot to the lower elementary building, and I was allowed to pick out chapter books. My reading level was ahead of my classmates, and I got to pick those Magic Treehouse books and dinosaurs.

Pursuing what interested me helped me foster my interest in environmental science. Deciding what to do with our lives has much in common with Montessori philosophies and values. Since we have an aptitude for this, and it's interesting and can help people, that's what we should be doing, which I attribute to Montessori. Growing up with Spider-Man, I'm also a big believer that if you have the power, you have the responsibility to help people too.

One thing that I got from school was the social aspect. I formed close connections with my classmates and teachers, and that whole community aspect of it was vital in middle and high school. It also influenced my path because I learned that valuing my relationships just as high as academic and professional things was okay.

—**Braeden Allen, environmental engineer, graduate of NewGate Montessori High School**

Montessori is the best way to learn! At Barrie, Dr. Montessori's teaching styles were prevalent from day one. The material taught by the teachers helped me understand at a young age that self-motivated education and being more independent in thinking were the best ways to learn and grow. Also, the ability to call your teachers by their first names made them more approachable and available, which made learning exciting and fun.

After graduating from Barrie, I felt prepared for what lay ahead for me in college and working toward my master's. From my first class until my last, I was able to think for myself, learn from my mistakes, and, most importantly, take away the crux of a Montessori education, which was being more independent and not always having to rely on others to solve issues.

—**Madhavi Sabnis, marketing and customer support coordinator at IndiSoft, graduate of the Barrie School**

CHAPTER 19

Deciding on Montessori

Montessori prepares students not just for college but for life. They aren't overwhelmed by competition and stress. The Montessori environment emphasizes community and belonging, where students feel safe, valued, and inspired to pursue their passions.

One parent described her child's experience: "My child is always excited to go to school because he sees it as a second home. There's a tangible sense of family here—a feeling of care, compassion, and respect that extends beyond academics."

Montessori children develop strong social and emotional skills that serve them well throughout life. They learn how to collaborate with others, think critically, and adapt to a rapidly changing world.

MONTESSORI STUDENTS SPEAK FOR THEMSELVES

A visitor once asked a six-year-old student in a Montessori classroom, "Is this your class?" The child confidently responded, "No, but I work here."

Another student was asked whether it was true that Montessori students can do whatever they want. She replied, "No, we have a plan. But we do like what we do."

FREQUENTLY ASKED QUESTIONS

Why do Montessori classes group different age levels together?

Montessori classes are organized to encompass a two- or three-year age span, which offers younger students the inspiration of older children, who in turn benefit from serving as role models. Each child learns at her own pace and is ready for any given lesson in her own time, not on the teacher's schedule of lessons. In a mixed-age class, children can always find peers who are working at their current level.

Children stay in the same class for three years. With two-thirds of the class returning each year, the classroom culture tends to remain stable.

Working in one class for two or three years allows students to develop a strong sense of community with their classmates and teachers. This age range also allows gifted children to be stimulated by intellectual peers without requiring them to skip a grade or feel emotionally out of place.

Why are Montessori classes larger than those in other schools?

The best teacher of a child is often a slightly older child. This process is good for both children. The larger group size puts the focus less on teachers and encourages children to learn from one another.

By consciously bringing children together in larger, multiage class groups, in which two-thirds of the children return each year, the school environment promotes continuity and the development of a stable community.

Why do Montessori schools ask young children to attend five days a week?

Since a primary goal of Montessori is creating a culture of consistency, order, and empowerment, most Montessori schools expect children to attend five days a week.

Why is Montessori so expensive?

Montessori programs require extensive teacher education for certification, as well as purchasing the educational materials and beautiful furniture that equip each Montessori classroom. All of this costs money.

Montessori is not always more expensive, though. Tuition costs depend on many factors, such as a particular school's size, buildings and grounds, teacher salaries, programs offered, and whether the school receives a subsidy payment from a sponsoring church, charity, or government agency.

Why do Montessori schools want children to enter at age three?

The early childhood Montessori environment for children aged three to six is designed to work with the characteristics of this stage of their development.

Learning during these years comes spontaneously, without effort. Montessori helps children to become self-motivated, self-disciplined, and to retain a sense of curiosity that so many children lose along the way in traditional classrooms. They tend to act with care and respect toward their environment and one another. Students work at their own pace and ability. The experience tends to nurture a joy of learning that prepares them for further challenges.

This process works best when children enter a Montessori program at age two or three and stay at least through kindergarten.

How can Montessori teachers meet the needs of so many different children?

Dr. Montessori believed that teachers should focus on the child as a person, not on a daily lesson plan. Montessori teachers lead children to ask questions, think for themselves, explore, investigate, and discover. Their ultimate objective is to help their students learn independently and retain the curiosity, creativity, and intelligence with which they were born.

Montessori teachers do not spend much time teaching lessons to the whole class. Their primary role is to prepare and maintain the physical, intellectual, and social-emotional environment. A key aspect of this is selecting intriguing and developmentally appropriate learning activities to meet each child's needs and interests.

Montessori teachers closely monitor their students' progress and use the children's interests to enrich the curriculum and provide alternative avenues for accomplishment and success.

Why is a Montessori classroom called a Children's House?

The Montessori classroom is not the domain of the adults in charge. It is a carefully prepared environment designed to facilitate the development of children's independence and sense of personal empowerment.

This is a children's community. Even very small children are responsible for the care of their own child-sized environment.

What do Montessori schools mean by *normalization*?

In the process of normalization, young children, who typically have a short attention span, learn to focus their intelligence, concentrate their energies for long periods of time, and take tremendous satisfaction from their work.

Is Montessori for all children?

The Montessori approach has been used successfully with children from all socioeconomic levels, representing those in mainstream classes as well as gifted students, those with developmental delays, and those with mental and physical disabilities.

There is no one school that is right for all children. Some children may do better in a smaller classroom setting with a more teacher-directed program that offers fewer choices and a more consistent external structure.

Is Montessori opposed to homework?

Most Montessori schools do not assign homework to children below the elementary level. When it is assigned to older children, it is meaningful, interesting assignments that expand on topics they are pursuing in class. Many assignments invite parents and children to work together. When possible, teachers provide opportunities to choose from several assignment options.

Is Montessori unstructured?

Montessori students live within a cultural context that requires the mastery of essential skills and knowledge, while them the opportunity to investigate subjects of particular interest. This environment allows them to set their own schedules during class time.

At the early childhood level, external structure is limited to clear-cut ground rules and procedures. By age five, most schools introduce some sort of formal system to help students keep track of what they have accomplished and what they still need to complete.

Elementary Montessori children usually work with a written study plan for the day or week. It lists the tasks they must complete while allowing them to decide how long to spend on each and what order they would like to follow. Beyond these tasks, children explore topics that capture their interest and imagination.

Are there tests in Montessori programs?

Montessori teachers carefully observe their students at work. They give their students informal, individual oral exams or have the children demonstrate what they have learned by teaching a lesson to another child or giving a formal presentation. Students also prepare their own written tests to administer to their friends.

Very few Montessori schools test children under the first or second grades. However, most schools regularly quiz elementary students on the concepts and skills that they have been studying. Older students in many schools also take annual standardized tests.

Although standardized tests may not offer a terribly accurate measure of a child's basic skills and knowledge, test-taking skills are just another practical life lesson that children need to master.

How do Montessori schools report student progress?

Because Montessori believes in individually paced academic progress, most schools do not assign letter grades or rank students according to their achievement. Student progress may be measured by student self-evaluations, portfolios of student work, student-parent-teacher conferences, or narrative progress reports.

Will my child be able to adjust to traditional public or private schools after Montessori?

By age five, Montessori children tend to be curious, confident learners who look forward to going to school. They are engaged, enthusiastic students who want to learn and ask excellent questions.

There is nothing inherent in Montessori that causes children to have a hard time if they transfer to traditional schools. Some will be bored. Others may not understand why everyone in the class has to do the same thing at the same time. But most adapt to their new setting fairly quickly, making new friends and succeeding within the definition of success understood in their new school.

Is Montessori opposed to competition?

Montessori is not opposed to competition on principle; Dr. Montessori simply observed that competition is an ineffective tool for motivating children to learn and work hard in school.

In Montessori schools, students learn to collaborate. They discover their own innate abilities and develop a strong sense of independence, self-confidence, and self-discipline. For an education to touch children's hearts and minds profoundly, students must be learning because they are curious and interested, not to earn the highest grade in the class.

Montessori schools allow competition to evolve naturally. The key is the child's voluntary decision to compete rather than having it imposed on him by the school.

Is it true that Montessori children never play?

All children play! They explore new things, watch something of interest with a fresh, open mind, enjoy the company of treasured adults and other children, make up stories, dream, and imagine.

Montessori students also tend to take their schoolwork quite seriously. They work hard and expect their parents to treat them and their work with respect. But it is joyful, playful, and anything but drudgery.

Is Montessori opposed to fantasy and creativity?

Fantasy and creativity are important aspects of a Montessori experience. Classrooms incorporate art, music, dance, and creative drama throughout the curriculum. Imagination plays a central role as children explore how the natural world works, visualize other cultures and ancient civilizations, and search for creative solutions to real-life problems.

What's the big deal about freedom and independence in Montessori?

Children learn best by doing, which requires movement and spontaneous investigation. Montessori children are free to move about, working alone or with others at will. They may select any activity and work with it as long as they wish, so long as they do not disturb anyone or damage anything, and as long as they put it back where it belongs when they are finished.

The prepared environment of the Montessori class is a learning laboratory in which children are allowed to explore, discover, and select their own work. The independence they gain is not only empowering on a social and emotional basis, but it is also helps them become comfortable and confident in their ability to master the environment, ask questions, puzzle out the answer, and learn.

What if a child doesn't feel like working?

While Montessori students are allowed considerable latitude to pursue topics that interest them, this freedom is not absolute. Every society has cultural norms and expectations for what a student should know and be able to do by a certain age.

Experienced Montessori teachers know these standards and provide as much structure and support as needed to ensure that students live up to them. If a child needs time and support to be developmentally ready, Montessori teachers provide it without judgment.

What about children with special needs?

Every child has special gifts, a unique learning style, and characteristics that can be considered special challenges. Montessori allows students to learn at their own pace and is quite flexible in adapting to different learning styles.

Many children with physical or learning disabilities may do very well in a Montessori classroom setting. Others do much better in a smaller, more structured classroom. Each situation must be evaluated individually to be sure a program can successfully meet a child's needs and learning style.

Wasn't Dr. Montessori's Method first developed for children with severe developmental delays?

The Montessori approach evolved over many years as the result of Dr. Montessori's work with different populations and age groups. One early group of children had been placed in a residential care setting because of severe developmental delays. The Method is used today with a wide range of children, but it is most commonly found in settings designed for populations without disabilities.

Is Montessori effective with highly gifted children?

Yes, in general, highly gifted children will find Montessori intellectually challenging and flexible enough to respond to them as unique individuals.

Is Montessori elitist?

No. Montessori is an educational philosophy and approach that can be found in all sorts of settings. In general, Montessori schools consciously strive to create and maintain a diverse student body, welcoming families of every ethnic background and religion, and using scholarships and financial aid to keep their school accessible. Montessori is also found in magnet public school programs, Head Start programs, and charter schools.

Does Montessori teach religion?

Except for those schools associated with a particular religious community, Montessori does not teach religion. Many Montessori schools celebrate holidays that are religious in origin but can be experienced on a cultural level as special days of family feasting, merriment, and wonder.

We do present great moral and spiritual themes, such as love, kindness, joy, and confidence in the fundamental goodness of life, in simple ways that encourage the child to begin the journey toward being fully alive and fully human. Everything is intended to nurture within the child a sense of joy and appreciation of life.

IS MONTESSORI RIGHT FOR OUR FAMILY?

Montessori is right for a wide range of personalities, temperaments, and learning styles. Children who consistently wait for adult direction and those who have difficulty choosing and staying engaged in activities may have some initial difficulty transitioning into a Montessori class, but they usually learn to trust themselves and gradually strengthen their concentration.

Parents who are particularly concerned about high standards and achievement may find Montessori difficult to understand and support. While we all want the best for our children, Montessori represents a different way of thinking, compared with most schools.

Montessori schools believe that children are normally born intelligent, curious, and creative and that all too often, parents and schools make the process of learning stressful rather than natural. We do not believe that most children need external or artificial structure and pressure to learn. We also believe that the current emphasis on testing and a state-established curriculum ignores common sense and the true nature of how children learn.

Montessori is right for families with a range of communication styles and learning expectations. However, families who are generally disorganized may experience frustration in a Montessori setting. The program is carefully structured to provide optimal learning opportunities for children. There is a place for everything, and everything is (generally) in its place! Children from somewhat chaotic families often cling to this structure and find it very reassuring. That said, the transition from home to school and back home again can be difficult.

Parents who are comfortable with Montessori tend to agree with the following basic ideas about education.

- Intelligence is not rare among human beings. It is in children from birth. With the right stimulation, reasoning and problem-solving skills can be nurtured in young children.
- Children are born curious, creative, and motivated to observe and learn things.
- The most important years of a child's education are the first six years of life. Infant and early childhood education are the foundation of everything that follows.
- It is important for children to develop a high degree of independence and autonomy.
- Academic competition and accountability are not effective ways to motivate students. Students learn more effectively when school is seen as a safe, exciting, and joyful experience.
- A competitive classroom environment stifles creativity.
- There is a direct link among children's sense of self-worth, empowerment, self-mastery, and their ability to learn and retain new skills and information.
- Education should be a transition from one level of independence, competency, and self-reliance to the next, not a process of passing exams and completing assignments.
- Children learn in different ways and at different paces. The idea that those who learn quickly are more talented misses a basic truth about how children really learn.

- Children learn best through hands-on experience, real-world application, and problem-solving.
- Teachers should serve as children's mentors, friends, and guides, not disciplinarians. Students should be treated with profound respect, not with condescension, external control, or domination.
- Children are capable of making choices to guide their own learning.
- It is helpful for children to work together on school projects.
- School should be a joyful experience.
- Our children will likely do well, and we are fairly relaxed about academic issues. We want school to be exciting and fun, not demanding and stressful.
- We want a school that will stimulate and encourage our child's curiosity, creativity, and imagination.
- Our family would like to stay at Montessori through the elementary program and perhaps beyond.
- Our family would like to be involved with our children's school and participate in as many school activities and events as possible.

Parents who feel comfortable with Montessori tend to disagree with or question statements such as the following.

- Academic competition prepares students for the real world.
- Children learn more when they are pushed.
- Testing helps to ensure accountability for children, teachers, and schools.
- Teachers must maintain strict discipline in the classroom.
- School should be like military boot camp, a place to earn a degree. It is not supposed to be fun.
- Our family places a very high priority on achievement.
- We want to ensure that our child gets into the best schools and colleges.
- Our family is able to attend some functions, but we have other commitments. It will depend on the event or function.
- Our family plans to stay in Montessori for a year or so to give our children a good start, and then we plan to transfer them to a different school.

Parents visiting a school for the first time

CHOOSING THE RIGHT MONTESSORI SCHOOL

Although most schools try to remain faithful to their understanding of Dr. Montessori's insights and research, they have all been influenced by the evolution of our culture and technology. Remember, the name Montessori refers to a method and philosophy. It is not protected by copyright or a central licensing or franchise program. In many parts of the world, anyone could, in theory, open a school and call it Montessori without knowledge of how an authentic program is organized or run.

One sign of a school's commitment is its membership in a professional Montessori society, such as the Association Montessori Internationale, the American Montessori Society, or the International Montessori Council. These groups and several other Montessori organizations offer schools an opportunity to become accredited.

As tempting as it can be to enroll without visiting a classroom, you will learn a great deal by spending thirty minutes to an hour watching the children at work. Ask permission to watch a work period first. Next, stay for a group meeting or come back later to watch one.

The following lists provide guidelines of what prospective families should look for when visiting Montessori schools.

The Montessori Learning Environment

- Montessori classrooms should be bright, warm, and inviting, filled with plants, animals, art, music, and books. Interest centers will be filled with intriguing learning materials, mathematical models, maps, charts, international and historical artifacts, a class library, an art area, a small natural science museum, and animals that the children are raising.
- You will not see rows of desks, a teacher's desk, or an electronic whiteboard. The environment will be set up to facilitate student discussion and stimulate collaborative learning.
- Montessori classrooms are organized into several curriculum areas, including language arts (reading, literature, grammar, creative writing, spelling, and handwriting), mathematics and geometry, everyday living skills, sensory-awareness exercises and puzzles, geography, history, science, art, music, and movement. Each area will be made up of shelf units, cabinets, and display tables with a wide variety of materials.

- Each class should contain the full complement of Montessori materials considered appropriate for this level.
- The furniture will be the right size for the students.
- Few, if any, toys are in a Montessori preschool classroom. Instead, a lovely, extensive collection of learning materials will match the developmental capabilities, interests, and needs of the children in the class.
- The learning activities should involve inquiry and discovery and provide continuous feedback on the student's progress. With older students, there should be evidence that multiple perspectives and differing viewpoints are treated with respect.

Class Composition

- A Montessori program is composed of mixed-age groups of children within each classroom, traditionally covering a three-year span. The levels correspond to the developmental stages of childhood: infants (birth through eighteen months); toddlers (eighteen months to three

years); early childhood (three to six years); lower elementary (six to eight years); upper elementary (nine to eleven years); middle school (twelve to fourteen years); and high school (fourteen to eighteen years).

- Ideally, a Montessori class has twenty-five to thirty students, balanced in gender and age.
- Montessori schools consciously work to attract a diverse student body and follow a clear non-discrimination policy.

Teachers

- Each class should be led by at least one teacher who holds a recognized Montessori credential for the age level taught.
- Each class includes either a second certified Montessori teacher or a paraprofessional teacher's assistant in addition to the lead Montessori teacher.
- Teachers generally work with one or two children at a time, advising, presenting a new lesson, or quietly observing the class at work.
- Montessori teachers should be respectfully engaged with their students.
- Teachers inspire, mentor, and facilitate the learning process more than they give lessons.

The Children at Work

- Students should feel at ease as they select and pursue activities. They should feel comfortable and safe.
- Students are typically scattered around the classroom, working alone or in small groups.
- Children and adults should interact respectfully. If there is conflict, teachers facilitate a resolution by guiding children to express their concerns and work together to find a solution.
- The focus of the class should be on children's learning, not on teachers' teaching.

During your visit, talk openly with school administrators and teachers, observe children working in a classroom, and ask questions such as the following.

- In what ways do you see Montessori as being different from other school programs?
- In what ways do you think your school is different from other Montessori schools in the community?
- What do you consider to be the school's strengths?

- Are there any areas of the school that you think need additional resources or attention? How are those being addressed?
- How would you describe a successful learner at this school?
- What sorts of children might not be as successful in this school?
- What do most parents who are pleased with this school find most appealing?
- Are there any values or expectations that might prevent this school from being a good fit for a particular family?
- If we were to apply to this school and be accepted, what advice would you give us to make it a wonderful experience for our child?
- What opportunities does this school provide for parents to become involved in their children's education? What expectations does the school have for us as parents?

The most important question in selecting a Montessori school is to consider how well it matches the education you want for your children. No one educational approach will be right for all children. The decision to enroll a child in a particular school should be based on the parent's and school's mutual belief that this will be a good fit for the child's personality and learning style, as well as the family's values and goals.

In determining which school is the best match, you will need to trust your eyes, ears, and gut instincts. Nothing beats your own observation and experience. The school that receives raves from one parent may be completely wrong for another.

Find a school that you love, and once you do, remember the old adage: "It is not a good idea to try to fix something that is already working." Some parents try different schools for a year or two and then move on to another. They do it with the best intentions, but children who are educated in one consistent approach and grow up within one school community tend to be more grounded and get more long-term value from their school experience than those who have to adjust to several different schools.

In the end, the selection of a Montessori school comes down to a matter of personal preference. If you visit a school and find yourself in love with the school's atmosphere and you can imagine your child happy and successful there, then that school is likely to be a good fit.

Concluding Thoughts

Dr. Montessori had a large vision for education—the establishment of universal and lasting peace. Although she witnessed two world wars and the unleashing of nuclear power, Dr. Montessori evolved a living philosophy of education child-study methods, age-appropriate curricula and instruction, and programs for adult teacher education. She recognized that schools tend to focus on teaching facts and skills without helping students see the bigger context of their place in human history and our role in shaping the future.

Man masters almost everything but himself . . . He avails himself of the most hidden treasures but does not use the immense riches and powers that lie within himself . . . This points to the great and urgent task of education! . . . If the school takes upon itself the task of mobilizing the young for the achievement of that perfect development that brings forward man as he can and is destined to be: conscious of the society he will become part of, master, not slave, of the infinite means that civilization puts at his disposal; equally developed in his moral and social powers as in his physical and intellectual ones; aware of his task, which requires the collaboration and unanimous effort of the whole of humanity—nobody will be overlooked.

Nobody will be rejected; nobody will be exempted! The whole of humanity will be enrolled in this service, which is a service for peace. Thus, education will become a true and invincible armament for peace! All human beings will grow to be "knights of peace" during that period . . . of formation when the cornerstones of the human personality are definitely fixed.

—Dr. Maria Montessori

"A NATION AT RISK"

The Montessori Way, with its focus on children's unique capabilities, stands in marked contrast to the directions of national education efforts. Back in 1981, the United States Department of Education established the National Commission on Excellence in Education. Its purpose was to study the quality of education in the United States and make recommendations for improvements.

The Commission's findings were published in 1983. Their report, titled "A Nation at Risk: The Imperative for Educational Reform," alarmed the nation and set a course of action that continues to dictate educational policy many years later. Although the opening paragraphs have been repeatedly reprinted, it is worth reading them again. Its emotional language stands in marked contrast to the convictions we call the Montessori Way.

The report was a call for mobilization. Educational improvements since 1983 have included investments in new curriculum, increases in salaries, incorporating technology into daily instruction, and the implementation of national, state, and local curriculum and assessment standards.

Despite studies of the human brain and new understandings of optimal learning conditions, the focus of school reform has, in our opinion, mainly been misdirected. Instead of accomplishing the comprehensive educational reforms that Dr. Montessori called for in 1940—creating schools based on partnership, community, and a joyful, natural approach to learning—during the past two decades, teachers and school administrators are now held accountable for their students' learning, which is increasingly measured by their performance on high-stakes tests.

Our nation is at risk. Our once unchallenged preeminence in commerce, industry, science, and technological innovation is being overtaken by competitors throughout the world. This report is concerned with only one of the many causes and dimensions of the problem, but it is the one that undergirds American prosperity, security, and civility. We report to the American people that while we can take justifiable pride in what our schools and colleges have historically accomplished and contributed to the United States and the well-being of its people, the educational foundations of our society are presently being eroded by a rising tide of mediocrity that threatens our very future as a nation and a people. What was unimaginable a generation ago has begun to occur — others are matching and surpassing our educational attainments.

If an unfriendly foreign power had attempted to impose on America the mediocre educational performance that exists today, we might well have viewed it as an act of war. As it stands, we have allowed this to happen to ourselves. We have even squandered the gains in student achievement made in the wake of the Sputnik challenge. Moreover, we have dismantled essential support systems, which helped make those gains possible. We have, in effect, been committing an act of unthinking, unilateral educational disarmament.

—"A Nation at Risk"

We believe that the national focus on children's test scores has too narrowly defined the purpose of education and the scope of learning experiences. This approach has created an inadequate definition of success for children. Consequently, it has led to an education system with reduced expectations for how children can and should grow and develop.

Along with many other educational philosophies, scientists, and developmental psychologists, we argue that the continuing tendency to hold schools and teachers accountable simply does not and will not work. Despite the considerable financial investment, teacher training, alignment of instruction to national, state, and local curricular standards, and teaching children how to test, children have yet to show much test score improvement.

Sadly, accountability measures have introduced fear into the learning environment by imposing sanctions on schools that do not meet targeted test scores. School board meetings become political battlegrounds. Teachers feel disrespected and insecure, contributing to a growing teacher shortage. Older generations of teachers are retiring or leaving the profession, while younger adults are reluctant to pursue a field perceived as undervalued and highly criticized, with limited opportunities for financial and professional growth.

The landscape of schools has drastically changed during this same historic period. With growing migration in many countries, today's schools educate children from numerous linguistic and cultural traditions, including those with an extensive range of learning challenges and styles in regular classrooms. At the same time, many schools are more stressful than ever before. They cope with growing levels of student mental health issues, including anxiety, depression, eating disorders, and school violence.

Education reforms have also included efforts to teach children how to reason and understand, identify and solve problems, work in teams, and communicate effectively.

These skills are said to help prepare children for adulthood in an information-age twenty-first century. Our children will face known problems with as yet unknown solutions: dwindling, nonrenewable energy supplies, climate change, environmental

degradation, global conflicts, pandemics, and even concern over artificial intelligence. Most children are awash in social media. They are exposed to misinformation, ceaseless commentary on their lives (online bullying), addictive media feeds, pornography, and other content that they often find difficult to navigate.

A DIFFERENT PHILOSOPHY

We find that the Montessori Way is more relevant today than ever before. Throughout this book, we have used the term Montessori to refer to a person, a philosophy, an understanding of how children learn, an educational method, a set of learning materials, and a way of life. This way of life is a philosophy for how human beings ought to live their lives and treat one another. It is an attitude of respect and encouragement for each human being, no matter how young or old. It is a sense of partnership rather than power and authority.

We argue that these are indeed the qualities of a fulfilled and happy life; these are the qualities of a person who is able to engage in today's pressing issues and challenges.

The Montessori Way recognizes that each child (and each adult) has their own unique capabilities. Each child has genius. A primary purpose of education is to help each child attain their full potential. The adult's task is to overcome their biases and prejudices and learn to see clearly the possibilities within each child. We assist children by preparing learning environments with carefully designed activities that allow them to exercise and develop their capabilities.

The practice of testing children to evaluate adult performance is wrong. The premise of supposing that test scores measure learning is limiting.

Children learn in relationships that nurture and support. Learning is a community experience, and trust between people is essential. Threats of loss of funds and public embarrassment elevate fear and lower trust. The learning community becomes fragile. The classroom, rather than the nation, is now at risk. Teachers and principals are frightened by the loss of jobs. Teachers pass on their fears and worries. Learners cannot engage in creative and critical-thinking skills when fear is present. As children become stressed, they cannot test well.

As American students' scores on both international and local accountability exams showed minimal gains, schools responded by better preparing children to take tests. Teachers teach "to the test." Students are drilled; memorization, not learning how to identify and solve problems, occupies lessons.

Schools make time for this by eliminating instructional time for art, music, recess, and physical education. In some schools, time for history and science has been reduced, if not eliminated. Time for test practice allows no time for students' interests or authentic problems.

A FACTORY-MODEL APPROACH

Teaching to the test is based on a factory-model approach to learning, a model that misunderstands and misuses children's learning capabilities and promises. In a factory, controls are implemented to ensure a uniform and quality product. While this process is important for material objects, it is inappropriate and wrong for children. Becoming the same is not the purpose of life.

An email that came out when we wrote the first edition of this book adds an interesting perspective. The widely shared email described a company's struggle to develop, market, and sell a unique product. The concept design was exciting, and this unique product met a national need. The marking plans were creative, innovative, and ready for release. According to the company's strategic business plan, there should have been no problem with generating huge profits. They had a winner. Everyone was excited and enthusiastic. This was a great place to work.

However, problems soon arose in the manufacturing process. The company was unable to consistently produce products that met manufacturing standards.

After careful study, the company's leaders determined that the source of the problem was its workforce. To correct this, the company reformed its policies to hold all employees accountable for measurable goals. Failure to produce would result in termination. For a while, more products were acceptable. But fear was rising. As leadership focused on faulty products and dismissed workers, the company's workplace culture continued to erode.

A new study was commissioned, and the company realized its problems came from its raw materials. Because this was a unique product, no one vendor could supply all of the needed raw materials. And because many vendors had to be involved, the raw materials needed to be standardized. Consequently, the materials would not have the same inherent properties and would not respond to one manufacturing process.

Leadership was in a quandary. They knew multiple manufacturing procedures would be required, but this would require considerable workforce training and an expensive retooling process. The leadership decided to cover up the results of its new study and focus, as before, on developing stronger accountability standards.

The email concluded by identifying the "company" and its unique product—American schools and the process of educating our children.

While we are not aware of any cover-ups in our school system, we are terribly mindful of the costs of not paying attention to each child's unique capabilities and learning approaches.

A test score, at best, indicates a specific performance or the child's response to specific test questions on a given day, which is easily affected by their health and emotional state. When it is finally reported weeks or months later, a test score is an artifact.

Caution should guide any decisions and conclusions based on test scores. Children have continued to learn and grow since the test date. Discussion about who they were and what they did masks who they are now and what they are capable of today.

The Montessori commitment to respect each child honors the learning process each child must follow as they make meaningful sense of knowledge and skills. Learning takes place every day and every waking moment. It happens uniquely for each child.

CURIOSITY, INQUIRY, AND EXPLORATION

In keeping with the principles of the Montessori Way, we imagine children will graduate from Montessori schools demonstrating the following characteristics.
- Initiative
- Creativity
- Imagination
- Conceptual thinking
- Curiosity
- Effort
- Irony
- Judgment
- Commitment
- Nuance
- Goodwill
- Ethical reflection
- A passion for learning
- The ability to choose and engage for long periods in personally fulfilling work

- The ability to identify a social problem and contribute to its solution
- Knowing how to respect and restore the natural environment
- An understanding of cultural and racial differences as a call for celebration rather than a cause for fear
- Self-discipline and responsible choice

We honor and respect individual children for their particular approaches and styles of learning. We help children develop habits and skills of lifelong learning with natural systems—curiosity, inquiry, and exploration—without resorting to external rewards, threats, and competition. Why do human children suddenly require learning goals in the form of measurable content standards to demonstrate that they learn? The argument, of course, is more political and, therefore, more controlling. It's not a question of learning; it's a question of who wants children to learn what.

Parents and teachers should investigate their state and local content and achievement standards, which are available on department of education websites around the world. These impressive lists of objectives hide the fact that real learning does not follow a neat and orderly progression. The focus must be larger than what is learned and include an understanding of how and when a child learns. In sum, we must learn to ask, "At this moment, who is learning what—and how?"

Dr. Montessori's approach to instruction is called *scientific pedagogy*. Montessori teachers act as research scientists and endeavor to understand the complete child to help facilitate the process of educating the human potential. Children are not taught; they learn. Teachers do not teach. They show, model, encourage, and create situations and conditions for children to investigate, inquire, and discover. In sum, children, not teachers, build knowledge. Children do not develop or learn uniformly at the same standard pace.

Children only learn when they can. A child will talk, walk, and balance a bicycle only when she is ready. A child will understand numbers, operations with fractions, equivalencies between geometric figures, and causes of historical events only when she is ready. A child will blend visual symbols for language ($c + a + t$) and read only when she is ready.

Not knowing today (as measured by a low test score) is not the same as not knowing forever. Similarly, knowing today (a high test score) does not guarantee knowing always. Humans do forget.

Dr. Montessori discovered the importance of repetition in a child's learning process. In her day, school involved recitation and memorization. Teachers spoke, and children recited back what they heard. In Montessori classrooms, children learn from repeated explorations of materials.

With repetition, children increase their understanding of concepts and improve their skills. This is as true for young children learning to arrange and sequence a set of cylinders of varying lengths

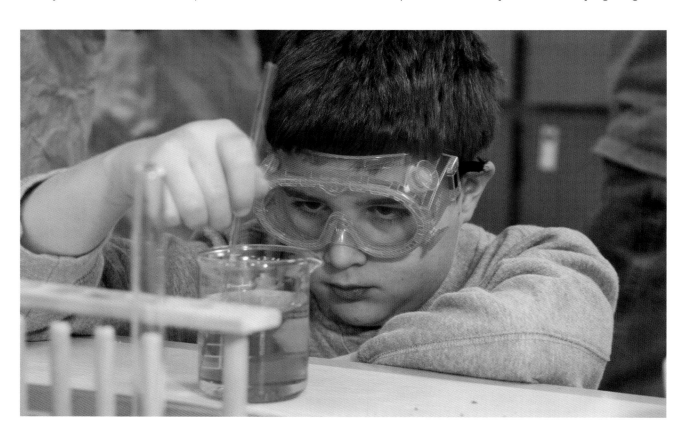

and diameters as it is for secondary students learning to research and present a persuasive essay or a proposal to improve local recycling efforts.

Education reform is as necessary today as it was at the start of the twentieth century. The current direction is too narrow and, because they are based on political agenda rather than children's development, too dangerous. Each child deserves a complete education in which all of their unique capabilities are engaged.

PREPARING FOR THE FUTURE

In today's rapidly changing world, a Montessori education holds unprecedented importance. As technological advancements continue to reshape our lives, the need for adaptability, creativity, and critical thinking has never been greater. Montessori education excels in fostering these skills through its emphasis on hands-on learning, problem-solving, and independent exploration. By nurturing a love for learning and the ability to adapt to new situations and challenges, Montessori prepares children for a future where many of the jobs they will hold do not yet exist.

Moreover, our awareness of mental health issues among children is increasing. Montessori's vital focus on social-emotional learning helps children develop resilience, empathy, and strong interpersonal skills, which are essential for mental well-being. Montessori classrooms encourage collaboration and community building, fostering a sense of belonging and interconnectedness that is crucial for personal and professional growth.

Technology, including modern media, has given everyone a voice and access to incredible amounts of information and disinformation. More than ever, people of all ages must find their own voice, meaning, and connection.

Research consistently shows that the quality of our relationships significantly impacts our mental health and has a direct correlation with human happiness. Many schools create conditions that make it difficult to form genuine community and relationships. Students may have many acquaintances but only a handful of friends. And many of those friendships are less than satisfying and authentic.

In the face of growing environmental concerns, Montessori education's emphasis on nature and environmental stewardship is particularly relevant. It instills a sense of responsibility and respect for the planet. Hands-on activities that involve caring for the environment and understanding ecological systems help children develop a practical and empathetic approach to sustainability, which is crucial for the future of our planet.

Montessori education's holistic approach to learning integrates various subjects, showing children how they interconnect and apply to the real world. The emphasis on practical life skills prepares children for everyday challenges, equipping them to handle a variety of situations.

Inclusivity and diversity are also fundamental to the Montessori philosophy. Children learn to appreciate and respect different perspectives, fostering a more harmonious and understanding society. The universal principles of the Montessori method can be adapted to various cultural contexts, making its value globally relevant.

Finally, the effectiveness of Montessori education is backed by extensive research. Numerous studies have shown that Montessori education promotes academic achievement, social skills, and emotional well-being. This evidence-based approach provides reassurance to parents and educators about its value.

Montessori education equips children with the necessary skills, attitudes, and knowledge to navigate and thrive in an ever-changing world. Its focus on holistic, individualized, and adaptive learning makes it a valuable and relevant educational approach for the twenty-first century. The principles and practices outlined in *The Montessori Way* emphasize the profound impact Montessori education can have, preparing children to meet the challenges and opportunities of the future with confidence and competence.

Selected Bibliography

This curated list of resources, primarily drawn from North American sources, represents some of the most important titles, in the authors' opinion.

Davies, S. (2019). *The Montessori toddler: A parent's guide to raising a curious and responsible human being.* Workman Publishing Company.

Davies, S. (2021). *The Montessori baby: A parent's guide to nurturing your baby with love, respect, and understanding.* Workman Publishing Company.

Davies, S., & Uzodike, J. (2024). *The Montessori child: A parent's guide to raising capable children with creative minds and compassionate hearts.* Workman Publishing Company.

De Stefano, C., & Conti, G. (2023). *The child is the teacher: A life of Maria Montessori.* Other Press.

Eissler, T. (2009). *Montessori madness!: A parent to parent argument for Montessori education.* Sevenoff, LLC.

Hainstock, E. G. (1997). *Teaching Montessori in the home: The preschool years* (Rev. ed.). New York, NY: Plume.

Hainstock, E. G. (1997). *Teaching Montessori in the home: The school years* (Rev. ed.). New York, NY: Plume.

Isaacs, B. (2018). *Understanding the Montessori approach* (2nd ed.). New York, NY: Routledge.

Lawrence, L. (1998). *Montessori read and write: A parents' guide to literacy for children.* New York, NY: Crown Publishing.

Lillard, A. S. (2016). *Montessori: The science behind the genius* (3rd ed.). Oxford: Oxford University Press.

Lillard, P. P. (1996). *Montessori today: A comprehensive approach to education from birth to adulthood.* New York, NY: Schocken.

Lillard, P. P., & Jessen, L. L. (2003). *Montessori from the start: The child at home from birth to age three.* New York, NY: Schocken.

McFarland, J., & McFarland, S. (2010). *Montessori parenting: Unveiling the authentic self.* Buena Vista, CO: Shining Mountain Press.

Montanaro, S. (1991). *Understanding the human being: The importance of the first three years of life.* Mountain View, CA: Nienhuis Montessori USA.

Montessori Jr., M. M. (1992). *Education for human development: Understanding Montessori* (Ed. P. P. Lillard). Oxford: Clio Press.

Montessori, M. (1912). *The Montessori method: Scientific pedagogy as applied to child education in "The Children's Houses."* New York, NY: Schocken.

Montessori, M. (1914). *Dr. Montessori's own handbook.* New York, NY: Schocken.

Montessori, M. (1917). *The advanced Montessori method* (Vols. 1-2). New York, NY: Schocken.

Montessori, M. (1932). *Peace and education.* New York, NY: AMS.

Montessori, M. (1936). *The child in the family* (Trans. N. Rockmore Cirillo). Oxford: Clio Press.

Montessori, M. (1936). *The secret of childhood: A book for all parents and teachers* (Trans. B. Barclay Carter). New York, NY: Ballantine.

Montessori, M. (1946). *Education for a new world.* Oxford: Clio Press.

Montessori, M. (1948). *Child education*. Adyar, Madras, India: Kalakshetra Publications.

Montessori, M. (1948). *The child*. Adyar, Madras, India: Theosophical Publishing House.

Montessori, M. (1948). *Reconstruction in education*. Adyar, Madras, India: Theosophical Publishing House.

Montessori, M. (1948). *The discovery of the child*. New York, NY: Ballantine.

Montessori, M. (1948). *To educate the human potential*. Oxford: Clio Press.

Montessori, M. (1949). *The absorbent mind* (Trans. C. Claremont). New York, NY: Henry Holt & Co.

Montessori, M. (1955). *The formation of man* (Trans. A. M. Joosten). Oxford: Clio Press.

Montessori, M. (1973). *From childhood to adolescence*. Oxford: Clio Press.

Montessori, M. (1997). *Basic ideas of Montessori's educational theory: Extracts from Maria Montessori's writings and teachings* (Comp. P. Oswald & G. Schulz-Benesch). Oxford: Clio Press.

Moudry, S. (2019). *Toilet awareness: Using Montessori philosophy to create a potty learning routine*. Self-published.

Moudry, S., & Moudry, J. P. (2019). *First foods to family meals: Help your child to prepare and enjoy food with your family*. Self-published.

Murray, A., & Debs, A., et al. (Eds.). (2023). *The Bloomsbury handbook of Montessori education*. London: Bloomsbury Academic.

Preschlack, P. (2023). *The Montessori potential: How to foster independence, respect, and joy in every child*. Chicago, IL: Chicago Review Press.

Rambusch, N. M. (1998). *Learning how to learn: An American approach to Montessori (Rev. ed.)*. New York, NY: American Montessori Society.

Schmidt, M. (2019). *Understanding Montessori: A guide for parents* (2nd ed.). Charleston, SC: CreateSpace Independent Publishing Platform.

Seldin, T. (2017). *How to raise an amazing child the Montessori way* (2nd ed.). New York, NY: DK Press.

Seldin, T., & McGrath, L. (2021). *Montessori for every family: A practical parenting guide to living, loving and learning*. New York, NY: DK Press.

Stephenson, S. (2003). *Michael Olaf's essential Montessori* (2 vols.). Arcata, CA: Michael Olaf Montessori Company.

Stephenson, S. M. (2019). *The red corolla: Montessori cosmic education*. Arcata, CA: Michael Olaf Montessori Company.

Stephenson, S. M. (2021). *Aid to life: Montessori beyond the classroom*. Arcata, CA: Michael Olaf Montessori Company.

Stephenson, S. M., & Lillard, A. S. (2017). *Montessori and mindfulness*. Arcata, CA: Michael Olaf Montessori Company.

Wolf, A. D. (1980). *A parents' guide to the Montessori classroom*. Altoona, PA: Parent Child Press.

Wolf, A. D. (1982). *The world of the child*. Altoona, PA: Parent Child Press.

Appendix

CURRENT RESEARCH IN SUPPORT OF MONTESSORI AND BRAIN DEVELOPMENT

By Dr. Angela Murray and Dr. Ann Epstein

We have been involved in Montessori research for over two decades and welcome this opportunity to summarize some recent developments.

We both contributed to the recently published *Bloomsbury Handbook of Montessori Education*, a comprehensive reference containing an entire section on the science of Montessori education. With sixty-two chapters, more than 600 pages, and almost 100 authors from more than twenty-five countries, we know most people will not read the handbook from cover to cover. We would like to highlight some of its research, which we've organized by questions we often hear.

Does Montessori education work?

While giving a one-word answer to this question is impossible, evidence supporting Montessori education continues to grow. A chapter in the handbook discusses the challenges of conducting rigorous research on Montessori education, summarizes global evidence, and concludes that current studies largely demonstrate Montessori's efficacy in promoting academic outcomes, executive function, and social-emotional skills (Manship, 2023).

Two recent articles that formally reviewed current research support these findings. One article found Montessori education more effective in developing cognitive abilities, social skills, creativity, motor skills, and academic achievement (Demangeon et al., 2023). Another concluded that Montessori education produces more positive results for general academic ability (math and language), inner experience of school, executive function, and creativity (Randolph et al., 2023). One author concludes, "Montessori education has a meaningful and positive impact on child outcomes, both academic and non-academic, relative to outcomes seen when using traditional educational methods" (p. 2).

Does Montessori education support social-emotional learning and other developmental outcomes?

Researchers are examining Montessori principles associated with nurturing social (or socio-emotional development and learning. Skills include being aware of and managing one's own emotions (especially when they are strong), understanding others' emotions, demonstrating kindness, and offering support when others are experiencing strong emotions (Crowder et al., 2019). Manship (2023) reported that young children in Montessori programs scored higher on social problem-solving tasks, demonstrated more positive playground behaviors, and had an increased ability to understand the perspectives of others. Manship also cited research findings that Montessori-educated children expressed greater creativity than same-age peers in traditional preschool settings in both the United States and France. Other areas showing positive impacts of Montessori education include social maturity and reduced anxiety in elementary students. Manship concludes, "Overall, the evidence that the Montessori method is effective at supporting social-emotional and other outcomes supportive of learning is notably consistent" (p. 214).

Montessori is an education for the senses and for developing close, trusting relationships between children and their teachers.

Is Montessori education outdated?

Since Montessori education has been around for more than one hundred years, skeptics often assume it must be outdated. On the contrary, modern science is discovering new ways to demonstrate how and why the Montessori approach continues to serve children so well today.

Neuroscience. Two European authors summarized their neuroscience work. Fabri (2023) connects current neuroscience to Montessori's ideas about critical periods, the importance of the environment, the role of emotional stimulation, the process of language acquisition, and the impact of movement on learning. Denervaud (2023) describes how she uses measures of behavior, brain structures, and neural responses to show that Montessori students are better able to detect and self-correct errors at an early age. She concludes that Montessori students have a healthier relationship with making mistakes when compared to students from traditional schools, likely because the approach encourages learning from errors rather than avoiding them.

Executive functions. Cognitive science and quantitative psychology are other modern fields offering evidence that Montessori education

is relevant today. Specifically, Mallett (2023) describes how Montessori education supports the development of executive functions by offering students regular opportunities to practice executive functions, scaffolding executive function skills, having a holistic focus that includes social-emotional learning, and offering a differentiated curriculum with significant student choice and active learning experiences.

Intrinsic motivation. Lillard and her graduate student Basargekar (2023) explain how interrelated elements of Montessori practices reflect current theories about the development of intrinsic motivation. Recommendations for fostering intrinsic motivation are organized around themes clearly found in Montessori classrooms, including autonomy (through student choice, classroom order, and teacher guidance), competence (through classroom organization, emphasizing embodied cognition, and offering interesting work), and relatedness (through teacher warmth, offering interconnected work, including three-year age groupings, and fostering an atmosphere of security and interrelatedness).

What other research will be of interest to practitioners?

Montessori research continues to grow and address current societal issues and educational challenges. This section highlights recent articles of particular relevance to practitioners, published in the *Journal of Montessori Research*. The journal is a publication of the American Montessori Society, launched in 2015 with support from the University of Kansas Libraries. Among the sixty blind peer-reviewed articles published to date, we discuss several that address the current state of Montessori education and issues of diversity, equity, inclusion, and belonging (DEIB) in the context of Montessori principles.

State of the Field, a comprehensive international census conducted in 2022, concluded that 15,763 Montessori schools operate in 154 countries today, with approximately 9 percent being government-funded (Debs et al., 2022).

The global study undertook the ambitious task of identifying components of Montessori fidelity with broad international acceptance.

Montessori schools strive to attract a diverse faculty and staff.

These six elements emerged as essential aspects of Montessori education: clear evidence of the Montessori philosophy, mixed ages, trained teachers, materials, freedom of choice, and uninterrupted work blocks.

Lillard, Tong, and Bray (2023) continued ongoing investigations of racial and ethnic parity. Their study of 134 non-white and white preschoolers revealed that non-white children in Montessori settings scored significantly higher on indicators of executive function and social cognition as well as early academics (literacy and math concepts) than their non-white peers in "business as usual" preschool programs, suggesting Montessori education's potential to close the gap for historically marginalized children.

Public school teachers in Hawaii embraced the cosmic nature of Montessori learning to honor Indigenous cultural components while addressing state-mandated Western science standards. A common holistic and relational worldview, beliefs based on observable facts and intuition, and recognition of the spiritual and scientific world working together emerged as themes in this qualitative study by Schonleber (2021). Teachers and school leaders purposefully incorporated Montessori principles into their teaching practices over a planned three-year period. They noted the impact of timelines, emphasis on the natural world, and the great lessons in achieving their goal of creating a culturally restorative, decolonized science program.

Where does Montessori research go from here?

While it is exciting to see the progress in Montessori research over the past twenty years, more work remains. Evidence supports Montessori education's effectiveness, but more large and robust studies are needed, which will require significant funding.

We also need studies that will allow us to understand and communicate the mechanisms contributing to what is working.

Other significant challenges will require additional research in Montessori contexts, including understanding the needs of twenty-first-century families, development and education in the digital age, navigating a plurilingual society, and many others.

Conversations about how we, as a society, address the challenges of educating today's children are beginning to open the door to alternative approaches like Montessori education.

In a provocative piece entitled "Why the Time is Ripe for an Education Revolution," Angeline Lillard (2023) argues that it is time for a paradigm shift "away from teacher-text-centered learning and to highly structured instructional environments that support self-construction through limited free choice" (p. 1).

These conversations and the growing number of studies supporting Montessori education offer encouragement that Montessori educators will have increasing opportunities to serve a larger and more diverse population of children in the future.

The challenge will be meeting the demand for high-quality, experienced, and dedicated Montessori educators.

References

Crowder, M. K., Gordon, R. A., Brown, R.D., Davidson, L.A. & Domitrovich, C.D. (2019). Linking social-emotional learning standards to the WCSD social-emotional competency assessment: A Rasch approach. *School Psychology*, 34(3), 281–295. https://doi.org/10.1037/spq0000308

Debs, M., de Brouwer, J., Murray, A., Lawrence, L., Tyne, M., & von der Wehl, C. (2022). Global diffusion of Montessori schools: A report from the 2022 global Montessori census. *Journal of Montessori Research*, 8(2), 1–11. https://doi.org/10.17161/jomr.v8i2.18675

Demangeon, A., Claudel-Valentin, S., Aubry, A., & Tazouti, Y. (2023). A meta-analysis of the effects of Montessori education on five fields of development and learning in preschool and school-age children. *Contemporary Educational Psychology*, 102182. https://doi.org/10.1016/j.cedpsych.2023.102182

Lillard, A. S. (2023). Why the time is ripe for an education revolution. *Frontiers in Developmental Psychology*, 1, 1177576. https://doi.org/10.3389/fdpys.2023.1177576

Lillard, A., Tong, X. & Bray, P.M. (2023). Seeking racial and ethnic parity in preschool outcomes: An exploratory study of public Montessori schools vs. business-as-usual schools. *Journal of Montessori Research*, 9(1), 22–36. https://doi.org/10.17161/jomr.v9i1.19540

Long, T., Ferranti, N., & Westerman, C. (2022). Children with disabilities attending Montessori programs in the United States. *Journal of Montessori Research*, 8(2), 16–32. https://doi.org/10.17161/jomr.v8i2.18639

Murray, A., Daoust, C., & Mallett, J. (2021). Designing the Montessori coaching tool elementary rubric for early-career professional development. *Journal of Montessori Research*, 7(2), 25–67. https://doi.org/10.17161/jomr.v7i2.15866

Randolph, J. J., Bryson, A., Menon, L., Henderson, D. K., Kureethara Manuel, A., Michaels, S., Rosenstein, d. l. w., McPherson, W., O'Grady, R., & Lillard, A. S. (2023). Montessori education's impact on academic and nonacademic outcomes: A systematic review. *Campbell Systematic Reviews*, 19, e1330. https://doi.org/10.1002/cl2.1330

Schonleber, N. (2021). Using the cosmic curriculum of Dr. Montessori toward the development of a place-based indigenous science program. *Journal of Montessori Research*, 7(2), 12–24. https://doi.org/10.17161/jomr.v7i2.15763

Acknowledgments

In October 2003, the Montessori Foundation self-published *The Montessori Way*. Our goal was to compile a book that would introduce Montessori as clearly as the articles in our magazine for Montessori families, *Tomorrow's Child*.

The first edition was made possible by a generous contribution from Tony Low-Beer of Greenwich, Connecticut, who has been a pillar of support for our work at the Foundation. His contribution, along with the support of our friends at Quarto Press, has paved the way for this second edition. We want to express our deep appreciation to Mr. Low-Beer and his family for their invaluable support.

We would like to take this opportunity to express our deep appreciation to each and every one of you who played a part in bringing this book to life. Your contributions, whether big or small, have made a significant impact and we are truly grateful for your support.

We also want to acknowledge and express our deepest gratitude to our colleagues who contributed to *The Montessori Way*. They include Susan Tracy, who contributed her expertise and experience in crafting the chapter on infant-toddler Montessori programs. Likewise, we want to thank Dr. Ann Epstein, who updated the chapter on learners with exceptionalities, and Dr. Angela Murray, who, with Dr. Epstein, contributed the survey of research into Montessori education.

Finally, we want to thank each of the Montessori schools and families who contributed photographs to illustrate this edition.

About the Authors

PAUL EPSTEIN, PhD
International Speaker,
Consultant, and Author

Paul has worked in Montessori education for over forty years as an administrator, teacher, researcher, consultant, international speaker, and author. He has been a Montessori classroom teacher in early childhood, middle, and high school programs, as well as a university professor. He is a director of early childhood and secondary teacher education programs. Paul's most recent publication is *An Observer's Notebook: Learning from Children with the Observation C.O.R.E.*

ROBIN HOWE, EdD
International Speaker,
Consultant, and Author

Daniel Robinson (Robin) Howe began his Montessori career at the age of two at the Barrie School in Silver Spring, Maryland, which he attended through the eighth grade. Graduating from Dickinson College with two majors (Spanish and religion), he went on to earn a master's degree in bioethics from University of South Florida. After successfully pursuing a career in the restaurant industry, Robin returned to get certification from Palm Harbor Montessori School (AMS), then attended St. Catherine's University to earn his lower and upper elementary certification (AMS). He also attended NAMTA's Orientation to Adolescent Studies (AMI). Robin holds a doctorate in educational leadership from Argosy University and worked with the Montessori Foundation's management team at NewGate (the Foundation's lab school), serving as co-head of school and as a senior Montessori Foundation school consultant.

TIM SELDIN, MEd
President of the Montessori
Foundation and Chair of the
International Montessori Council

Tim Seldin's more than fifty years of experience in Montessori education includes twenty-two years as head of the Barrie School in Silver Spring, Maryland. Tim was the cofounder of the Institute for Advanced Montessori Studies and the Center for Guided Montessori Studies. He currently serves as the executive director of the NewGate School in Sarasota, Florida. He earned a BA in history and philosophy from Georgetown University; an MEd in educational administration and supervision from the American University; and his Montessori certification from the American Montessori Society. Tim is the author of several books on Montessori education, including *How to Raise an Amazing Child*; *Montessori for Every Family* with Lorna McGrath; *Building a World-Class Montessori School*; *Finding the Perfect Match: Recruit and Retain Your Ideal Enrollment*; *Master Teachers–Model Programs*; *Starting a New Montessori School*; *Celebrations of Life*; and *The World in the Palm of Her Hand*.

Index